# WHEN GOD IS FAR AWAY

## *Clinging to Faith in the Wilderness*

### VANESSA I. ODUAH

To contact the author:
38032 Postal Dr
Attn: Vanessa Oduah
Zephyrhills, FL 33542
cclpublishco@gmail.com

ISBN: 978-0-578-39541-8 (paperback)
ISBN: 978-0-578-39543-2 (eBook)
Library of Congress Number: 9780578395418

First paperback edition July 2022

**Printed in the United States of America**

# Dedication

To the Blue Angels of Hernando Correctional Institution- thank you for allowing me to share so many laughs and tears; hugs and songs; and hopes and dreams with you over the years. I pray that our moments together have been as invaluable to you as they have been to me. You are always in my heart.

To my brother, Patrick, I pray that you are proud of who I am becoming. May your face never fade from my eyes, may your voice never leave my ears, and may your memory never leave my heart.

# Acknowledgements

"…the Father of compassion and the God of all comfort" receives all the credit and all my gratitude for carrying me through darkness and filling me with words to share.

My son, Micaiah, is the beauty that God gave me for ashes. His life makes mine worth living, and he motivates me to achieve my goals.

Minister Barbara Thomas encouraged me to start writing and not stop until the book was complete.

My father, Chika, Daniel, Shanna, Courtney, and Chris reviewed my drafts and gave me feedback. Thank all of you for your time and concern.

# TABLE OF CONTENTS

# INTRODUCTION

Nine months after getting married, I filed for a divorce.

The following month, I found out that a tiny human had been growing inside me for the past five months.

Less than a month after that, my brother died alone in his apartment.

Nine months later, after having tried to repair my marriage, I filed for a divorce again.

How does all that happen to someone who trusts in God? What are you supposed to do when your life turns on its head and God completely vanishes?

How do you begin to search for God when He seems so far away, and do you even *want* to look for Him?

Before I go any further, I want to thank you for choosing to read this book. I am grateful that God has allowed you and me to connect in this way.

I hope that the words of this book speak to you in your season of life, whatever that may be. Perhaps you believe in Jesus Christ as Lord and Savior, but you feel like you are losing hold of Him. If your relationship with God is not where it once was or where you would like it to be, then I hope this book provides you with scriptural and practical ways to reconnect.

You may be experiencing great intimacy with God at this stage of your life. I hope that this book allows you to venture more deeply into that intimacy. May these words magnify the wonders of the God you love and can always run to in times of trouble.

If you do not yet have a relationship with Jesus Christ, I pray that this book becomes a resource to help you navigate the Holy Bible and understand what intimacy with God means. Maybe you have considered giving your life to Christ, but you do not know what that looks like in everyday life. You are not sure how things will change or what challenges you may face and if God will truly be there for you through each of them. I hope this book encourages you to pursue the single most important relationship you will ever have in this life.

I gave my life to Christ as a young girl, and, if I am honest, I had been sailing fairly smoothly ever since. I thought that, as a Christian, I deserved to have a peaceful and privileged life. I figured I had always been able to avoid major issues because I simply "did things right." I have had a relationship with God for as long as I can remember, but I was deceiving myself by giving way too much credit to my own efforts and devotion.

By the time I decided to write this book, that smooth-sailing ship had crashed headfirst into an iceberg. I was pummeled by one crisis after another, and it felt like God had exited, stage right, from my life. Among other issues, I was ending a tumultuous marriage, learning about my unborn baby halfway through my pregnancy, and coming to terms with the tragic death of my brother. Life was driving me to the brink. I was drowning; but crying out to God seemed to get me nowhere. Every day, I wrestled with the temptation to write Him off as either uncaring or incapable. My mind was urging me to handle these challenges myself, to act according to my feelings and not worry about the consequences. But if I listened to my mind, I would end it all. I was in a fight for my life, and the odds were not in my favor.

In the midst of the chaos, I somehow managed to hear God instruct me to continue visiting His "blue angels," women serving their sentences at Hernando Correctional Institution in Brooksville, Fl. I had been visiting them at least once a month for five years or so, mentoring, teaching, worshipping with and praying with them. It was easy to do this when things were going well for me. To go while barely hanging onto sanity was another story. But God was persistent. Not only did He want me to go; He told me to prepare a message that would address exactly what I was facing. I needed to translate my feelings of confusion and despair into spoken words. Then, He promised, I would find the answers to the questions I had been asking: Where was He? Why was I going through these things? How would I go on from here?

In spite of my hesitation, He filled my notebook with the message He wanted me to deliver. On a Sunday evening, I stood before my sisters, as I affectionately call them, and spoke. Crying and hugging myself to keep from doubling over, I know that only by God's strength was I able to get my words out. To my surprise and God's credit, many ladies came to me afterwards to thank and encourage me. I pray that I completed my assignment to God's satisfaction and that those words still resonate with the Blue Angels today.

Over the next few weeks, God delivered on His promise. I began to hear Him more clearly. I felt His comfort and was reassured that He cared about my life. A few months later, God instructed me to record that message in my first book. Thanks to Him, you are reading that book now.

There are seven chapters, representing the seven steps God took me through to find my way back to Him. Although each chapter builds upon the last, you should feel free to explore this book in the order that works best for you. Maybe you will find yourself starting from the end or reading a particular segment twice. Maybe one chapter will become more relevant in another season of your life. I encourage you to keep this book handy and reference it as often as needed. Take time with the reflections at the end of each chapter before moving on to the next. Most importantly, please delve into the scriptures that are referenced in parentheses. On their own, my words cannot connect you to God; only He can pull you to Him through *His* Holy word. I do not claim to have all the answers to life's challenges. This book is by no means an end-all-be-all resource or exhaustive how-to guide. I can only testify that these seven steps helped *me* through my battles. And now, it is my honor and privilege to share them with you.

Despite its limitations, I pray that this book provides you with applicable guidance to direct you in tough times. I pray you discover that you are well equipped to win, even in the middle of a fierce storm. And as you emerge from your wilderness, may you experience intimacy with God as never before.

# CHAPTER

*One*

## Recognize who God is

"I don't even know who you are anymore."

Have you ever said this to or heard it from someone? Whether you are the one saying or hearing it, it can be deeply painful. We all want to understand and be understood by the people we love most. But life has a way of bending and twisting relationships to the point that people we once thought we knew well suddenly feel like strangers. I do not think anything impacts a relationship like the unraveling of familiarity. Trust goes out the window, doubt creeps in, and walls go up. Sometimes, the relationship does not survive.

This does not happen only in our relationships with each other. Setbacks, curveballs, and tragedies can change the way that we perceive God and His nearness. God may seem far away from us, and we may begin to doubt the characteristics that we once associated with Him, like His kindness or power. We may begin to wonder if He truly is everywhere and all-knowing. Can He hear us when we cry at night or scream in frustration during the day? Does He really have everything under control? Maybe at one point, we have even said, "God, I don't know who you are anymore" or "I'm not interested in getting to know that God."

If you are like me, then it is easy to think of yourself as the center of God's universe when hard times come. I know I am not the only one who has ever asked, "Why is God being unfair to me?", "What did I do to deserve this?", or "What is the point of trying to be a good person if God is not blessing me?"

For a long time, I thought that I could avoid life's pitfalls and hardships if I just tried my best to do everything right. So, when life showed up at my door to take me for a wild ride without my permission, I was shocked to say the least! I hosted a luxurious pity party and invited my family and close friends. More than a few times, they tried their best to encourage me as I cried, "Why, God?? How could you, Lord?? I did x, y, and z, and you allowed *this* to happen??" Even though I had brought some of my crises upon myself, I was not letting God off the hook!

In those moments, I was thinking of myself more highly than I should have been. Have you ever found yourself doing this? Paul, an apostle of the early Christian church, cautioned believers in Rome against this kind of thinking (Rom. 12:3), and that warning still holds weight today.

But how can we not think that way when everything is going wrong? When trouble comes and we cannot sense God, it is almost natural for us to do a flip-flop between God and our circumstances. God becomes smaller in our minds, uncaring or incapable. Meanwhile, our circumstances become infinite and all-consuming.

When we are hit with crises or disappointments and God seems far away, I believe the first thing for us to do is recognize who He is. A friend of mine phrases this in a way that always resonates with me: *"If there's something about God that we don't understand, we need to stop, pull back, and focus on what we do understand."* Although God has not revealed His full essence to us, there is much that we *can* learn about Him, and we should hold onto these truths as we encounter the ups and downs of life.

## God is Sovereign

God has supreme, permanent authority on Earth and in heaven. He rules how He chooses, and- by design- we will never understand everything about Him in this life. That can be a hard pill to swallow! But rather than letting this agitate us, we can be comforted and reassured by how God *has* revealed Himself to us.

He has shown Himself to be the sole creator and everlasting keeper of the universe (Gen. 1:1, Rom. 1:20). He is a responsible manager of this planet (Gen. 8:22, Job 5:10, Psa. 19:1). He has proven Himself to be a knowledgeable regulator of our bodies, souls, and spirits (Ecc. 12:7; Mat. 6:25-32, 11:29; 1 The. 5:23). NOTHING can thrive, matter, or exist unless God does. He chooses to sustain our very existence day after day. If we take a moment to think about the innumerable tasks that God accomplishes every minute out of love for us, perhaps we can keep the tough seasons of life in perspective.

I proudly admit that I am old-fashioned. Although I am in my thirties, those close to me would probably describe me as closer to

73. According to them, one of my hobbies that makes me old-fashioned is doing jigsaw puzzles. A good 1000-piece can keep me locked away for hours!

As I am working through a puzzle, I usually pick up a piece that does not seem to fit anywhere. Its color, shape, or size may throw me completely off. I look intensely back and forth from the picture on the front of the box to the piece in my hand. Sometimes, I become frustrated and convince myself that the piece must have landed in the box by accident.

As I keep moving, I eventually get to a hole in the puzzle: four pieces connected by their corners but missing a central piece. Of course, that random piece that I had wanted to ignore is the exact and only piece that will fit. If I had had the opportunity to see the puzzle maker create the puzzle, perhaps I would be more careful to keep that random piece close by. It would be easier for me to trust that even though it seems out of place, and I cannot immediately figure out its purpose, the entire picture would be incomplete without it.

The Lord is an expert at putting puzzles together, and this universe is His kajillion-piece work of art. But unlike me, God also created the very pieces that He is putting together! And *we* are those pieces! Each of our lives; every aspect of nature; every idea, invention, and interaction are parts of God's puzzle. No one person can fully envision the complete picture or understand each of the intricate connections needed to get there. Even the tiny subsection of the puzzle that is one person's life can be utterly confusing. Are there moments or even years that do not seem to fit into what you thought your life would be? Who would not erase even a single moment of his or her past given the chance? A major mistake, turbulent trial, or heavy loss has probably made each of us feel that God was distant or non-existent at some point. But even if you did not understand the purpose of that moment- even if you *still* do not understand it- God does. He designed that seemingly ill-fitted puzzle piece and made it an essential part of your life picture. That is how His sovereignty works.

## We Can Never be Like God

Let's make sure that we come to terms with some truths that may be tough to digest. Whether you are just getting to know God or have an established relationship with Him, I believe everyone should live with the understanding that God is superior to us. Maybe, we can even find beauty within these truths. So, here are the big facts:

God and humankind will NEVER exist in equality. God is a unique being, and He belongs to a unique class that never accepts new members. He is, has been, and always will be the undisputed king of the universe. Period. God paints with colors that our natural eyes cannot see. He engineers sounds at frequencies that our human ears cannot detect. He provides food for creatures that we do not even know exist. The chasm that separates humanity's greatest accomplishments from God's is wider than the distance from the sun to Pluto.

We cannot grasp the span of God's wisdom, no matter how great our relationship may be with Him. Anyone who attempts to equate himself or herself with God is, at best, woefully confused. When it comes to our will versus God's will, His will wins (unless He chooses to defer to ours). If our "truth" stands in conflict with His, then our "truth" is a lie. God's opinions are never wrong, His purposes are never negotiable, and His laws are never debatable.

Whew! Are you still there? Are we all okay after that reality check? Let's take a moment together and allow all that to make its way deep down to the depths of our souls!

...Okay, let's keep going.

How can there be beauty in being subject to a God like that??

The beautiful thing about God's superiority is that we are not primarily responsible for the upkeep of this planet or even our own lives. Yes, God endowed us with authority, skills, and intelligence to fulfill specific purposes. And I am not suggesting that we are free to trash the earth! But can you think of any person you would trust to manage all that occurs on this planet? Even the manager of a three-employee business messes up from time to time! That type of management is outside of our ability- praise be to God for taking on the challenge with excellence and love!

Honestly, it can be difficult to acknowledge and submit to someone so much greater than we are. But God designed and desires us to be inferior to Him in every way. And if we think about it, this is how creation always works: the created should be less than the creator. Have you ever watched a movie with a robot or some other invention going rogue and trying to overtake the inventor? When that happens, we see the invention as the villain, because we all have an innate understanding that what was designed cannot be equal or superior to whoever designed it.

It is especially important to remember this when God seems far from us. Why? Because we all have a common enemy, whose name is Satan. And one of Satan's go-to tricks is to deceive us into believing that we somehow *can* exist in equality with God. He wants us to think that it is possible for a human being to be equal to or even greater than God. Need proof?

Let us visit Genesis 3, where we find Adam and Eve, God's first human creatures, face-to-face with Satan. He was trying to convince Eve to eat the fruit of a tree that God had expressly designated as off-limits. Eventually, she and Adam gave in to Satan's urging. But everything had been perfect up to that point. God had met all of Adam and Eve's needs. The three of them were in total sync. So, how did Satan persuade Adam and Eve to disobey God?

He did not insist that the fruit would taste great. He did not try to assure them that God would not notice. Satan had enough lies to fill a garden, but he selected this one: "You will be like God..." (Gen. 3:5). Satan convinced Adam and Eve that they could know what God knew, and he presented what appeared to be a guaranteed way to attain this unattainable knowledge. That lie entrapped the first man and woman, and it continues to entrap their offspring- all humanity. As soon as the couple ate the fruit, they were bombarded with revelations that they could not handle. And ever since then, we have all been weighed down by our useless attempts to explain what we can never fully understand in this life.

If we do not allow Satan to trick us with this lie, and we accept our status as imperfect, lost creatures in need of direction, then it becomes easier to embrace God in all His superiority. Surrendering the dark moments of our lives to Him is always worth the risk because He knows what to do with them.

## God does not Owe us Explanations

God loves you and me without question. But He does not answer *to* us, and He is certainly not obligated to provide every answer *for* us. Any response that God provides to our questions is an act of absolute grace. Sound harsh? Yeah, I know. But let us consider why God owes no explanations to anyone:

**1.** We have nothing of our own to offer Him. To be clear- when I say nothing, that is what I mean. Nothing. Zero items. Not one scrap of tangible matter or weightless substance. Now, before you go and read off a list of what you *do* have to offer God, remember that it should be a list of what you OWN. We tend to claim ownership of things and people- *my* body, *my* children, *my* idea, *my* purpose. And in a worldly sense, this is understandable. I do not believe that God is offended when we use the word "my." It helps us identify what we have obtained by conception, currency, or contract. Governments write laws around the concept of what is mine and what is yours. From person to person, "my" plays an essential role in conversation.

From person to God is another story. There is no need to assign people, places, or ideas to one side or the other, because they all belong on one side (spoiler alert: not ours). Every person on Earth was and will be created by God. Every place was carved from elements that God brought into existence. Every idea was developed in a brain that- you guessed it- God formed. The Holy Spirit often

12

reminds me that everything my eyes can see was created either by God or by someone who was created by God.

The only way that someone can legally take possession of something they did not create is to receive the right to ownership from the creator or someone acting on their behalf. God, who is the ultimate creator, has not given that right to any of us. What He *has* given us is guardianship, stewardship, and several incredible gifts. This is what is meant in the Bible when God uses words like "yours" or "I give it to you" (e.g., Gen 13:17). He does not mean it as something that you keep eternally (except for your salvation). Even your children and friends are not really yours. If you want to check me on this, call up your closest friend and politely ask if you can take him or her along with you to your grave when you die- just try not to be offended by their response! No one enters this world with anything but a naked body, and even *that* is eventually reclaimed by the dust, which God created!

The truth about what I own became very real to me when my brother, Patrick, died. At some point in my younger days, I had assigned myself the task of protecting my siblings with my life, because they are mine- or, so I thought. I believed that I could maintain their wellbeing if I always knew what was going on with them. As we began branching out from home, I always called and visited each of them whenever I could. I know that I was not wrong to check on them, and I still do that today. But my actions were giving me a false sense of ownership. So, when I received the call on that December evening, all I could say was, 'How could *my* brother die? He is *my* brother!' Believing that I had failed in what I thought to be my God-ordained assignment left me with a deep sense of aimlessness. What else was there for me to do in life if I had not been able to keep my brother alive? But I had to accept that Patrick's life did not belong to me or even to Patrick; it belonged to God. Although I impacted his life as his sister, God had created and sustained it all on His own. And that is why God did not ask for my opinion before deciding to call Patrick, someone *He* had created, home.

Since we have nothing to offer God, He has no existential reason to confide in us. Isaiah 40:13-14 asks, "Who has directed the Spirit of the Lord, or as His counselor has taught Him? With whom did He take counsel, and who instructed Him...?" We tend to confide in other people who can guide or provide for us. But for God, there is no such person. He lays this out rather bluntly in Psalm 50:12- "If I were hungry, I would not tell you; for the world is Mine, and all its fullness." Do not take this personally. It's not us, it's God. He is just that perfect. And that perfect God is madly in love with us!

**2.** We are not God's bosses. I often must remind myself that "He is God, and I am not." This means that all godly rights and privileges, like being the boss of everything and everybody, belong to Him. Maybe you are a parent, teacher, or employer who has had to remind someone under your guardianship or on your payroll that *you* are in charge. But just as it is with earthly ownership, earthly boss status is legitimate to an extent. It does not compare to what God has going on as THE boss. We cannot do absolutely everything that we want to do. No one can command everything in life to be a certain way. But God can. "I am God, and there is none like Me... And I will do all my pleasure" (Isa. 46:9-10). Take a second to internalize the fact that everything on Earth is here because God wanted or allowed it to be. (P.S. That includes you- God wants you here for a reason!)

Since we do not have supreme authority, there is no way we can demand that God do what we want Him to do. Nor can we force Him to block the challenges that come up against us. To be clear, this does not mean that we should sit idly and allow tough circumstances to defeat us without going to God. He *wants* us to come to Him; He *wants* us to talk to Him and ask Him for help. He is delighted to rescue and save us at any time. But how can we know the difference between questioning and challenging God, between talking to Him and complaining to Him?

God can handle our questions when we are confused or even agitated. He sent Moses, who would come to be one of Israel's greatest leaders, to demand that Pharaoh release God's people from slavery in Egypt. But Moses' first attempt seemed like a total failure: Pharoah flatly refused to release the Israelites. Afterwards, Moses asked God, "Why is it you have sent me?" (Exo. 5:22). And the Lord answered Moses, giving a guarantee that He would deliver the Israelites from Egypt (Exo. 6:1).

Contrast this with the way God handled complaints from the Israelite people (yes, the ones He had just delivered from Egypt). If you continue through the book of Exodus, you will find that God did not take too kindly to their murmurs and groans, and He handed out severe individual and corporate punishments. Perhaps the greatest consequence was the time it took the people to trek from Egypt to the promised land of Canaan. What would normally be an 11-day trip became a 40-year stay. Israel's complaining led to disobedience and idolatry, which so angered God that, more than once, He was prepared to annihilate them and blot them out from the face of the planet (Exo. 32:11-14; Num. 14:11-20)! If this was God's reaction to a few years' worth of complaints, imagine how He is faring with centuries of complaints now! Thank God for Moses stepping in as Israel's advocate and for Jesus Christ stepping in as ours! But even with such a faithful and gracious advocate, we may want to think twice before challenging God or complaining about how the borrowed lives that we live on this borrowed earth are going. We can always bring our concerns to Him humbly, but He has the freedom to respond in His own way. Sometimes, God may have to give us an abrasive reminder of who He is. For another example, let me take you to my favorite chapters in the Bible: Job 38-42.

To give you a bit of backstory, Job was a man who loved God and had an abundantly blessed life. He raised ten children with his wife, possessed a multitude of livestock, and was highly regarded in his community. Because of his devotion to the Lord, Satan asked God for permission to slam Job with back-to-back calamities. If that does not sound crazy enough, the Lord said 'Yes.' Yep, you read that right-God *allowed* Job to lose his wealth, good health, and children! All these tragedies hit Job with no warning or immediate comfort from the God he had diligently served for years. These were devastating circumstances even for a faithful man like Job. Cursing his very existence, he insisted that God hold a trial so that he could defend his innocence and receive an explanation for such hardship.

Through thirty-five chapters of the book, there is no recorded response from God. Imagine Job's frustration and hopelessness! His friends tried unsuccessfully to speak for God and provide the reason for Job's circumstances. Honestly, how could anyone explain being deeply intimate with God one minute and hearing not even a whisper from Him the next? What was the rationale behind Job's fall from bountiful wealth to abject poverty in a matter of days? No one was able to reveal God's mind to Job. And for thirty-five chapters, God provided no answers.

Then comes chapter 38, where we encounter what has to be the greatest response in recorded history.

God speaks from a whirlwind- that alone should have been enough to shut Job's mouth! He fires a string of unanswerable questions at Job, each intended to make unequivocally clear the distinction between the speaker and the listener. God takes Job to court as requested, challenging Job to brace himself and respond to the interrogation. By the end of the trial, Job is defenseless and contrite. He has no choice but to acknowledge that he had spoken without understanding and that God is indeed sovereign (chapter 42). Job comes to terms with the depth of his smallness and the danger of his arrogance; he can barely stand the thought of himself (42:8). Graciously, the Lord fills Job's later years with more children and abundance than he had had before.

I do not bring up Job's story to make us "despise" ourselves, as Job declared. But these events in Job's life highlight God's sovereignty over all things and people. Because God made us, He has the right to shower us with prosperity or sink us into poverty. It is His choice to bless us with good health or afflict us with illness. We do not always know His plan, but we can be assured of this: in time, it will bring good to us and glory to Him. The challenge that you are facing now may be tough and God may seem distant. But trust me- the outcome will be for your good! You may ask, "Even if things do work out for me in the end, what about the road *to* the end?" Would it not be lovely for God to lay out the blueprint and tell us what to expect every step of the way? Well, do not hold your breath, because He probably will not!

As I continue to figure life out, I find that the trick is not to be so preoccupied with what God has *not* yet revealed that I ignore what He *has* revealed. When I stress over what I do not know, it is easy for me to accuse God of being wicked or unfair. Agonizing over the "why" rather than moving confidently through the "what" while trusting in the "who" can land us in a dangerous place, where Satan is free to blur the lines between God and man. As evidenced in the book of Job and throughout the Bible, God will make those lines crystal clear for us if we do not learn to do so ourselves.

Life has left me with many unanswered questions, especially about my brother. *Why didn't God prevent his death? Why didn't he send me some sign that something was wrong? Why did He allow my brother to die alone?*

I have not received all the answers yet, and I do not know if I ever will in this life. But I must stop, pull back, and remind myself of what I know to be true about God: He loves my brother more than I ever could, and He has welcomed him into heaven with open arms. If I trust Him, then He will continue to give me strength to live in this new normal, where I must reach back into my memories to find Patrick. The strength and peace that God has given are more useful to me than the answers that He has withheld; for that, I am grateful.

## God is a Perfect Being

God's perfection is something else to keep in mind, but that is tough to do when it seems as though He does not see, hear, or care. It is also difficult to grasp because we rarely, if ever, encounter anything here on Earth that is perfect. We cannot relate God's perfection to anyone or anything else; we can only contrast it with the glaring imperfections of our own nature. Some people cannot handle such a contrast and reject God altogether on that basis. But if we believe that God exists and is who He claims to be, then we ought to embrace His perfection.

The Merriam-Webster dictionary defines perfection as being entirely without flaws or defects. This certainly describes the Lord. God is devoid of error in His person, principles, and purposes. This is important to remember because Satan would like us to believe otherwise. He would rather we be convinced, or at least suspicious, that God has made a mistake in the handling of our lives. Perhaps Satan has whispered in your ear that God is overlooking you. Maybe he has even told you that *you* are a mistake, and that God has no real plan for your life. Or perhaps he uses a more indirect means to deceive you, like a professor who scoffs at the idea of a divine and perfect being. Or a subtle joke on TV to poke fun at those who profess faith in Jesus Christ. I often hear people ask, "How can a perfect God allow all this evil in the world?" or "How come that perfect God could not cure my child's cancer?" These valid questions have legitimate answers that do not negate God's perfection, but Satan is intent on parading our suffering and God's goodness as two realities that cannot coexist. He wants us to take hold of the lie that God simply makes mistakes, like everyone else. But we have established that God is not like anyone else in the universe.

Perfection is also defined as excellence or completion beyond practical or theoretical improvement. Again, only God truly fits this description. We may try to conjure up our idea of a perfect god- likely just some hyped-up version of ourselves. We may even say, "If God was perfect, then He would…" The devil preys on this line of thought. Psalm 19, known as the perfect revelation of Yahweh (the Lord's personal name), tells us that God's law is perfect (19:7). But Satan's tactic is to convince us that God's laws require some scrutiny, if not a complete overhaul. If we revisit Adam and Eve in the garden of Eden, we find that Satan deceived Eve by suggesting that God's command about the tree was flawed. He wants to deceive you and me, also. Do not allow him to distort what you know to be true about God. If you are not utterly convinced that God is perfect, I challenge you to hold on to the possibility that He is. It will take you much farther than any myth that Satan can offer you.

## What's God's Deal, anyway?

Is God holding out on us? Does He take some sick pleasure in watching us flail about, trying to make some sense out of life? That is how the enemy wants us to think, particularly when we are facing challenges. He wants you to think that God is distant from you because He is holding out on you, and that you can do better about your situation than God can. Granted, Satan knows more than we do because he is impressively studious. But his acquired knowledge pales in comparison to God's innate omniscience. Satan's arguments against God are tainted with unwarranted blame, faulty premises, half-truths, and empty promises. But if we believe him, we may find ourselves falling deep into self-righteousness, fear, doubt, or resentment. Eventually, we may begin to distance *ourselves* from God.

The truth is, yes, God *is* holding some things back from us. Not out of wickedness, but out of love and wisdom. Imagine a kindergarten student marching up to the school principal one afternoon, demanding to know why she separated recess by grade level. The patient principal smiles, looking past the child's frown and raised voice. She softly responds, "Trust me- I designed it that way because it is the best thing for you and all the students in this school." God's response is often the same: a patient and loving reassurance that we can trust Him. He knows what He is doing, and He is always closer than we think.

You may be asking what God's perfection has to do with your imperfect life. How God executes His flawless purpose in an imperfect world through the lives of flawed people is a great mystery. Our lives will never be perfect at any point while we are on Earth. But God is adding, subtracting, multiplying, and dividing the circumstances of our lives, bringing solutions that align with HIS plan. God is bringing about a perfect kingdom, and He is allowing our imperfect thoughts, endeavors, and relationships to play major roles in this mission. God's plans for His kingdom and for your life are perfect - they are infallible, inerrant, and impossible to improve. I wish I could fully comprehend the intricacies of His plan, but it is beyond any human scope of understanding. Only in heaven will we see and understand all the things of God (1 Cor. 13:9-12). But even though God holds some things back from us, He continues to reveal so much to us. And we should be grateful for that. God is not a malicious dictator who shoves and maneuvers the pieces of our lives around with no regard for our hearts. No, God wants to share and discuss with us. He wants to let us in on the matters of His heart. He does not want us to follow Him blindly or by force. If God seems distant from you, remember these truths about Him. And then go and seek Him; He promises that you will find Him (Pro. 8:17).

# Reflections

1. What do I say and do to acknowledge that God is sovereign over the universe and over my life? Am I truly okay with this truth?

2. What characteristics do I believe are true about God? With which characteristics am I struggling?

3. How can I keep the truths of God's nature and sovereignty at the forefront of my mind and use them as weapons against Satan's lies?

4. (Read Revelation 19-22). Do these scriptures assure me of God's ultimate victory over all evil through Jesus Christ? How does this victory apply to my current challenges?

# CHAPTER

*Two*

## Put God's Word in its Place

I believe the greatest tool that God has given us is His word. With His words, God formed heaven and earth. His words dictate every aspect of our lives from beginning to end. Victory over Satan now and throughout eternity is promised and detailed in His word. Granted, Satan is well-versed in Biblical verse, and he constantly tries to discredit what God has said. But we can stay on the offense by keeping God's word in primary position, especially when He seems far away from us.

When I think about God's words, I place them into two categories-the universal and the specific.

What I consider the universal word is what is written in the Bible. Throughout each book, there are messages of hope, encouragement, justice, and love even amid strife, poverty, war, and struggle. The Bible is not a rose-colored nursery rhyme written just to make us feel warm and fuzzy (although it certainly can do that!). It is the revelation of a powerful and loving God who creates, destroys, blesses, curses, elevates, lowers, chastises, and saves humanity for His glory!

God's "specific" words are the messages that He customizes for every person. God cares for us so much that He takes time to speak to every one of us in a unique way. I struggle at times with cutting out all the background noise and grasping God's specific word for me. Other times, it is easy for Satan to trick me out of believing what God is telling me. Does this happen to you? Or maybe you are just figuring this whole God thing out and have no idea how to hear His words to you. Maybe you are not even sure that He talks to you.

One thing I know is this- if He has words for me, then He has words for you, too! And they are powerful, life-altering words that we can receive and apply every day.

## God's Universal Word

The Bible has been scrutinized, criticized, and cast aside for centuries. Growing up in a home with a strong Biblical influence did not stop me from asking questions like "Is it even real? Is it historically accurate? Is it all that useful?" But as I go through the peaks and valleys of life, as I recognize my weaknesses and inabilities, and as I aspire to live a fulfilled life, I am convinced that God's word is a must-have. No one can tell me that it is not the most effective weapon against the evils of the world. I have not encountered a person menacing enough, a prescription potent enough, a song melodious enough, or a church service riveting enough to compel Satan to wave the white flag and surrender forever. He can fight against our mindsets, medications, and even our ministry! It is the word of God, and the word alone, that continues to defeat Satan in battle.

Why?

Let me offer two reasons: 1- The Bible contains the only documented proof of Satan's inevitable destruction; and 2- The author of the Bible is Satan's master, the LORD God Himself.

God's Word is powerful, but how often do we overlook it and search for answers elsewhere? How many times have we substituted news outlets, horoscopes, medical remedies, or someone else's advice for the Bible in our battles against Satan? I don't know about you, but when I want excuses for myself or revenge for someone else, that Bible does nothing for me!

When we want guidance but cannot find God, we are in prime territory for Satan to come knocking with these distractions. To be clear, I am not saying that news outlets, medicine, or human advice are wicked or ineffective (horoscopes are another story). But they should not take the place of God's word. This, however, is exactly what Satan wants to happen. He wants us to believe that the Bible is at best obsolete, if not altogether untrue. Satan would rather be confronted with anything or anyone *other* than God's word, because he can handle anything and anyone else. We cannot allow him to rob us of the weapon that God has freely given us: the "sword of the Spirit" (Eph. 6:17).

So, what *is* in this Bible that holds so much weight against Satan?

## *His Identity*

Satan operates with anonymity. He cloaks himself with shadows and lands victories by painting himself as an imaginary being. This contradicts another trait of his- arrogance. We usually associate arrogance with people who demand excessive attention and strive to keep the spotlight on themselves. They like to let others know who they are and what they have done. But Satan is different. He cannot reveal exactly who he is because he is a loser- literally! He is all smoke and mirrors, so he masks his identity. Any coverup will do. Satan does not care if we believe he is our best buddy, king of the universe, or a villain from a fairy tale; he will wear all the costumes it takes to keep us unaware of his tactics. And if not been for that Bible, Satan would have gotten away with his charade just like the bad guy in Scooby Doo! (Admit it: Scooby Doo was a great show!)

The Bible unequivocally exposes both Satan's identity and his mission. Jesus told a crowd of listeners that Satan is the **father of lies** (John 8:44). Later, He referred to Satan as a **thief** who comes to "steal, and to kill, and to destroy." (John 10:10). Peter wrote that he is our **adversary** and that he seeks souls to devour (1 Pet. 5:8). Paul warned the Corinthian church that Satan disguises himself as an **angel of light**, setting an example for his followers to disguise themselves as "ministers of righteousness" (1 Cor. 11:14). According to Matthew's account, Jesus said that Satan snatches the word of the kingdom of God from those who hear but make no effort to understand it (Mat. 13:19). Christ's followers in the city of Ephesus were warned that Satan is a **spirit** working in the "sons of disobedience" (Eph. 2:2). Paul's second letter to the Thessalonians refers to him as the **lawless one** (2 The. 2:9).

Satan wants to take control of, or possess, the minds of Christ's followers. John 13:27 records how Satan entered the mind of Judas Iscariot, enabling him to carry out the plan that Judas had already concocted to turn Jesus over to his accusers. Unbeknownst to Simon Peter, Jesus' faithful disciple, Satan had once sought God's permission to take control of him (Luke 22:31). And in the Old Testament, Satan convinced King David to number the citizens of Israel when God had not authorized him to do so (1 Chr. 21:1). Although the Old Testament does not include as many direct references to Satan as the New Testament does, he is embodied in humans and nations, like the prince of Tyre (Eze. 28:1), the king of Babylon (Isa. 14:4), and false gods of the nations surrounding Israel (Jud. 10:6).

But the Bible gives us more than Satan's name and game. There are also indisputable, emphatic, and graphic declarations about his ultimate defeat! This is illustrated indirectly in the Old Testament as nations from near and far challenged Israel in battle. Although Israel was a tiny nation in terms of population size, the Israelites were God's people. And through them, God defeated Satan in battle countless times. The Moabites, Amorites, Jebusites, Sidonians, and Philistines were just a few enemy nations who came to learn that Satan had deceived them with hopes of victory on the battlefield. Additionally, Isaiah exclaimed that Satan fell from heaven, calling him by his heavenly name, Lucifer (Isa. 14:12). The Lord rebuked Satan from His presence and revealed this to the prophet Zechariah (Zec. 3:2). In fact, the Bible opens with God promising that Satan will have everlasting defeat (Gen. 3:15).

The New Testament lays out Satan's destruction more directly. According to John, the reason the Son of God appeared on earth was to destroy the works of the devil (1 John 3:8). When He was tempted by Satan, Jesus referred to the written word of God to run him off (Mat. 4:10). Before seventy of His disciples, Jesus shared His personal testimony, which corroborated that of Isaiah: He saw Satan fall "like lightning from heaven" (Luke 10:18). Paul assured the Romans that the God of peace would soon crush Satan (Rom. 16:20). Last but certainly not least, God gave the disciple, John, profound revelations of Satan's eternal defeat:

- **Rev. 3:9-** "Indeed, I will make those of the synagogue of Satan…come and worship before your feet."

- **Rev. 12:9-** "So the great dragon was cast out, that serpent of old, called the Devil and Satan…he was cast out to the earth…"

- **Rev. 19:20-** "Then the beast was captured, and with him the false prophet…These two were cast alive into the lake of fire burning with brimstone."

- **Rev. 10:20-** "The devil, who deceived them, was cast into the lake of fire and brimstone…And they will be tormented day and night forever and ever."

Failure is a guarantee for Satan, and he knows it. He knows he will lose the war and that God will dish out his perennial punishment. He even knows that he will lose the battles that he wages here on earth against God's children if we know what weapons to use against him! And our how-to guide for winning against Satan in battle is found in - you guessed it- God's word.

James advised believers in Christ to submit to God and resist the devil (Jam. 4:7). Paul warned specifically against harboring anger to avoid giving room to the devil (Eph. 4:27). In Paul's letter to the Corinthian church, we learn that forgiving others is a weapon against Satan (2 Cor. 2:5-11). Peter's guidance is for us to be "sober-minded" and "watchful" (1 Pet. 5:8). And the book of Ephesians gives us the "armor of God" as we stand against the devil (Eph. 6:10-18). Those who do not have a relationship with God through Jesus Christ are captive to Satan's power, but they can be released if they "open their eyes" and see Christ for who He is (Acts 26:18).

Jesus set an example for us to recognize and rebuke Satan, no matter whom he uses to approach us, when he chastised Peter for speaking against what the Father had already ordained to happen (Mat. 16:23).

Satan works tirelessly to keep us ignorant of this wealth of weaponry against him. If you are like me, you may underestimate the power of God's word when you cannot trace Him. But lack of faith in God's word will stand in the way of us defeating Satan. While we are searching for God, we must be on guard against messages that challenge or dismiss the Bible. They can come from anyone- a family member, friend, teacher, coworker, entertainer, or leader.

### *Our Identity*

God's word also gives us the full picture of our identity, and what a glorious picture it is! There is no positive thought, master class, or 12-step program that can compete with the Bible when it comes to affirming one's identity. I am not saying that positive thinking, master classes, and 12-step programs are never helpful; they may produce life-changing results. But none of these should be our primary source of affirmation. Only the word of God tells us the absolute truth about who we are. It was, after all, authored by our creator.

If Satan cannot deceive you about *his* identity, rest assured that deceiving you about *yours* is worth a try. Sadly, this is perhaps one of his most effective weapons against us. Millions of people- some followers of Christ, some not- live day to day with a false sense of identity. What is worse is that many people do not even *realize* that they do not know who they are.

I am not simply talking about knowing what you like and dislike, what career path you should take, or what gets under your skin. I am talking about understanding yourself at the fundamental level: a spiritual being housed in a physical body. A person created and most greatly desired by God. And a son or daughter of God if you follow Jesus Christ.

Let us look at what the Bible says about humankind:

- God made us in His image and named us Man (Gen. 1:26, 5:1, 9:6; Psa. 100:3).

- Some among Man are created as male and some are created as female (Gen. 5:2, Mark 10:6).

- Our breath is dependent upon God (Job 33:4).

- God created us to rule (Gen. 1:26-27).

- Out of all God's creation, we are positioned just below Him and crowned with glory and honor (Psa. 8:5, Heb. 2:7).

- God's Son, Jesus Christ, gave His life as a ransom to buy our souls back from Satan (1 Tim. 2:6).

- God created us to spread throughout the earth and worship Him as we diversify in complexion, culture, and currency (Gen 9:1; 10-11, Psa. 117; Dan 4:1-3, Acts 2:7-11, Rev. 7:9-10)

- God loves us (John 3:16, 1 John 3:1)!

Mankind is precious to God. We have power infused into our anatomy and glory embedded within our physiology. If we want to manifest that power and glory to maximize our humanity, we must go to the only one who grants us access to an abundant life: Jesus Christ (John 10:10).

Here is what the word says specifically about those who come to the Father through Jesus Christ:

- We belong to Christ, who belongs to God (1 Cor. 3:23).

- Each of us is a new creation (2 Cor. 5:17).

- God lives inside of us in the person of the Holy Spirit (1 Cor. 6:19).

- God considers us His children, and we can call Him Father (John 1:12, Rom 8:15).

- We are citizens of heaven (Phil 3:20).

- We have unlimited access to God's mercy (1 Pet. 2:10, Heb. 4:16).

- We are holy, royal, and chosen to share God's excellence with the world (1 Pet. 2:9).

- We are not slaves to sin anymore (Rom. 6:6).

- We are no longer sentenced to spend eternity with Satan and away from God (Rom. 8:1).

- We are the fragrance of Christ in the world (2 Cor 2:15).

- We light up the world (Matt. 5:14).

- We can do all things through Christ (Phil. 4:13).

- Jesus Christ unifies us (Gal. 3:28).

- God loves us (John 3:16, 1 John 3:1)!

If you have become accustomed to these words throughout your life, you may forget to appreciate the wonder and power within them. Or perhaps you are coming across these scriptures for only the first or second time. Whatever the case, I encourage you to take some quiet time, digest each scripture, and search the Bible for more, since this is by no means a complete list. I pray that you realize or remember that you are God's treasure. Nobody can deny God's love for you, not even Satan. Scriptures like these are the last things that Satan wants us to come across when we are struggling to find God's presence in our lives. For his lies to ring as truth- lies that we have no place in God's plan or that sins and mistakes will forever weigh us down- these scriptures must be false. In fact, Satan may be satisfied if we believe that they apply to everyone *except* us. If he can get us to believe that *we* need to be more righteous, kind, or devout to receive God's gifts of salvation and adoption, then he will defeat us time after time. Do not give him that ammunition. Believe and proclaim these words for yourself!

### *God's Written Promises*

As children of God, we are entitled to many promises from our Father. These promises apply to our lives even when God seems far from us. God is not like us; He does not make promises that He cannot or does not intend to fulfill. His faithfulness will not allow Him to go back on His word. Encourage yourself and stand against Satan's lies with these scriptures:

- All things work together for our good according to God's purpose (Rom. 8:28).

- Whatever darkness or distress comes our way, we can conquer it (Rom. 8:37).

- The world brings trouble, but Christ has overcome the world (John 16:33).

- God will give us rest if we come to Him with our burdens (Matt. 11:28, 1 Pet 5:7).

- The Lord fights for us (Exo. 14:14).

- We overcome Satan by the blood of Jesus Christ and our testimony (Rev. 12:11).

- God has good plans for us (Jer. 29:11).

- God helps, strengthens, and upholds us (Isa. 41:10).

- Trials that feel like rivers and fires will not conquer us (Isa. 43:2).

- Weapons that anyone designs to use against us will fail (Isa. 54:17).

- God does not withhold good things from those who walk like Him (Psa. 84:11).

- God restores our health and heals our wounds (Jer. 30:17).

- The Lord is always around to help us in trouble (Psa. 46:1).

No matter what the world thinks of God's written word, it is our most reliable manual for life and most effective weapon for the battles we face. Ingesting God's Word and applying it to our lives also increases our faith and draws us closer to Him.

## God's Spoken Word

The Bible is not the only place where we should search for God's words. He speaks specifically into the life of every person He creates, including you! When God is hard to trace, it is important to hold firmly to His word concerning your life. Perhaps He has given you a vision of a focused and purposeful life, but right now you are still struggling to find your way. Maybe you and your spouse are trying to conceive the child He showed you in a dream. Or maybe you have been suffering in an abusive relationship, but He has assured you a way out. Maybe He has promised to deliver you from an addiction. Perhaps it is a promise concerning your education, career, or health. Whatever He has spoken to you, the writer of Hebrews tells us that He is faithful to fulfill it (Heb. 10:23).

Why is it important for us to know and internalize what God has declared about each of us individually? Because we live by "every word that proceeds from the mouth of God" (Deu. 8:3, Mat. 4:4). God's word should sustain and navigate us. But when we do not hear or feel close to Him, it can be tempting to chart our own path. Sticking to God's plan can become even more difficult when unexpected issues and hardships arise that seem to run in complete contrast to what we thought God said. We may ask ourselves, *why trust God's plan for my life if He is not showing up in it? If I am going to run into trouble whether I am following God's path or not, then why stress myself out trying to trust Him? I am going to do what I think is best for me.*

This line of thinking is easy to buy into. The problem, however, is that there *is* someone out there who *does* believe what God has said concerning you, and it is the same enemy we have been talking about! He knows that God is fully capable of fulfilling every letter of every word that leaves His mouth. Satan was once with God in heaven (called Lucifer then), so he has seen God's majestic and sovereign rule with his own eyes. He was on Earth, witnessing firsthand the manifestation of God's words in Genesis 1. Satan heard God use His words to bring the sun, mountains, birds, and humanity into being. So, whether Satan knows that God's word is potent and fruitful is not the question; he absolutely does. He wants *you* to believe that it is *not*.

I usually find it much harder to believe God's specific word concerning my personal life than His written words to all believers. The Bible has been recorded, copied, and translated into hundreds of languages. But the word that He gave to *me*, for *me* - where is that? Even if I write it down, who can vouch for it if it has not yet taken place?

God's specific word for your life probably will not thunder from heaven among a crowd of listeners who can testify to hearing it with you. You may receive it through a sermon, a dream, or time in prayer. And this may be all that you have to go on for days, months, or even years before it actualizes. How can you hold onto what may have been nothing more than a whisper in your ear and allow that to navigate the course of your life? Only one way- by faith.

Three times in the Bible, we are advised that just (or righteous) people live by faith (Hab. 2:4, Rom. 1:17, Heb. 10:38). And Paul told the believers in Rome that faith comes when we hear the Word (Rom. 10:17). (In this context, "hear" is understood as spiritual hearing that picks up God's voice.) Applying these scriptures to our lives looks like this: when we receive words from God, either universal or specific, we keep them in the forefront of our minds and use them daily as the absolute authority over the area of our lives to which they pertain.

Let us consider some biblical examples of people who had faith in God's specific message, even when the circumstances made the message seem impossible.

- **Abraham and Sarah** were promised a son and many generations after him. God had talked with Abraham about this at least three times in Abraham's life: when he was 75, about 85, and 99 years old. Time, however, seemed to be running against God's word. The couple even tried to bring the promise to reality in their own way. But they turned back to trusting God, and they gave birth to a son when Abraham was 100 and Sarah 90 years old (Gen. 12-21).

- When **Joseph** was around 17 years old, God sent him two dreams foretelling a great position that he would hold in the future, when people would bow before him. He made the mistake (or so it seemed) of sharing his dreams with his brothers, who then sold him into slavery in Egypt. From slavery, Joseph spent 13 years in prison, having committed no crime. But he continued to trust God, and at long last he was released and became second in command over all Egypt. True to those teenage dreams, even his father and brothers came and bowed before him! (Gen. 37-48)

- **David** was a teenager (most likely 15 or 16 years old) when God directed the prophet Samuel to anoint him as king of Israel. But there was *already* a king at the time, and he began to resent young David, who was rising in prominence. Before making it to the throne, David faced battles and numerous attempts on his life. He hid in caves and even pretended to be insane just to stay alive. But God kept His promise, and the Israelites crowned David as king at 30 years old. Even though he had spent years of his life on the run, David never lost hope in God. (1 Sam. 16- 2 Sam. 5)

- **A poor, widowed mother from the town of Zarephath** was visited by the prophet Elijah during a harsh drought. She told him that she had barely enough flour left to make one last meal for herself and her son before they died. Elijah responded by asking her to sacrifice that pittance of flour to make *him* a cake, which must have sounded severely obnoxious! But he promised the woman that her flour and oil would not run out before God ended the drought. The woman abandoned human reason and obeyed Elijah, showing her faith in God. After that, her household was able to eat "for many days." (1 Kin. 17:8-16)

- Elijah's successor, Elisha, stayed with **a well-to-do woman from the town of Shunem** and her husband. When Elisha asked how he could repay the woman for her kindness, he learned that she had long desired a son. He then received a word from God and relayed it to her: she would give birth to a son the following year. The woman was skeptical at first; but as promised, she gave birth the following year. Some years later, the boy suddenly became sick, so sick that he died in his mother's lap. With a measure of faith that gave her incredible strength, the woman traveled to Elisha to tell him that her son had died. On the way, she told both her husband and Elisha's servant "It is well," despite her son lying lifeless in the house. Elisha returned to her house and prayed, and God restored the boy's life. (2 Kin. 4:8-37)

- **Mary and Joseph** were a young, betrothed couple (they had entered a covenantal agreement to be married but had not yet consummated the marriage) when an angel of God visited Mary. He delivered a promise that, by the Holy Spirit, she would give birth to a son who would reign on King David's throne and save God's people from their sins. This confounded Mary, who was not only a virgin but a betrothed woman in a society that did not take kindly to sex before marriage. When Joseph found out that she was pregnant, he planned to end the betrothal privately. But an angel revealed to him what God was doing through Mary. The couple undoubtedly had to deal with scoffs and murmurs within their community as Mary's belly grew. Yet, they stayed together and trusted God's plan. And the rest is Jesus! (Mat. 1:18-25; Luke 1:26-38)

- Jesus told his disciple, **Peter**, that he would die an old man (John 21:17-19). A short while later, after Jesus had returned to heaven, King Herod arrested Peter and threw him in jail for preaching the gospel. This same king had just murdered James, another disciple of Jesus. Bound in chains and monitored by two guards, Peter seemed to have few worries. He fell asleep as if he was home in his bed! Peter must have remembered Jesus' promise, and that was enough to reassure him that his incarceration was both temporary and durable.

Thank God for these vivid examples of living by faith! Despite barrenness, poverty, persecution, death, and biological impossibilities, these and countless other ordinary people held on to the word that God had given them (Heb. 11:4-38). Now, God wants to add your and my victories to His record. Will we take the time to receive a message from Him concerning our lives? Will we treasure that message and hide it in our hearts? Finally, will we walk and live as if God has already delivered on the promise?

If you do not know what God has promised you specifically, and He seems too far away for you to receive any message from Him, then stand on His written words to all believers. These promises are no less powerful or important than His customized, individual promises. Whether it is for you alone or for the entire body of Jesus Christ, keep God's word on your mind, lips, hands, and feet. Rest assured that heaven and earth will pass away before any fragment of God's word fades (Mat. 5:18, 24:35, Luke 21:33).

# Reflections

1.  What will I do this week to become more familiar with God's universal Word?

2.  What do I find hard to believe about God's universal or specific words? How may Satan be taking advantage of my skepticism?

3.  Where do I go to look for answers or hope other than to God's word? Do these alternate resources give me clarity and spur me to faith-based action?

4.  Does my understanding of my identity contradict with who God has said that I am?

5.  Does any person in my life dismiss the Word of God? If so, what actions do I need to take to reject what they are saying?

6.  What do I know or think God has promised specifically for me? Do I believe that it will happen? If so, how is my daily life reflecting my belief? If not, what person in biblical history had an experience most like mine and trusted God through it?

# CHAPTER

## Three

# Put Your Feelings in Their Place

Let's talk about something that everyone either absolutely loves or absolutely hates to talk about: our feelings. Regardless of age, sex, ethnicity, or experience, feelings are universal. Everyone's feelings are important, and we should explore and express them in appropriate ways. This chapter is not intended to help you dismiss, suppress, or reject your emotions. Instead, let us think about how we regard and respond to our feelings.

Our feelings have a place in God's heart, plans, and kingdom. Once I began to understand the relationship between God and my feelings, I became closer to Him and started experiencing victories in areas of my life where I had previously failed. This chapter follows the chapter about God's word to illustrate what I have learned about life as a follower of Christ: God's word comes before our feelings. Always. Full stop.

Our feelings are **REAL** and **RELEVANT**, but they should not **RULE** our thoughts and actions.

## Our Feelings are REAL

We all have feelings. Culture may influence them, experiences or disorders may stifle them, and counseling may expose them; but they exist within each one of us. God engineered and implanted feelings into us; they are a core component of our humanity. Human beings did not imagine feelings into existence; that gives us too much credit! It is not we but God who is the creator of feelings. Believe it or not, God has feelings, too! When God the Father, God the Son, and God the Holy Spirit came together to create humans in their likeness (Gen. 1:26), they included emotions in the blueprint, because each of them has emotions. God's emotions are part of what makes Him a person (not a human).

Dive into the scriptures for examples of God expressing His feelings:

- John 11:35- "Jesus **wept**."

- Proverbs 6:16- "There are six things the LORD **hates**, yes, seven are an abomination to Him."

- Zephaniah 3:17- "The LORD your God in your midst...He will **rejoice** over you with **gladness**."

- Deuteronomy 9:8- "Also in Horeb, you provoked the LORD to **wrath**, so that the LORD was **angry** enough to have destroyed you."

- Psalm 149:4- "For the LORD takes **pleasure** in His people..."

- Numbers 14:34- "…for each day you shall bear your guilt one year, namely forty years, and you shall know My **displeasure**."

- Ezekiel 16:42- "So I will lay to rest My **fury** toward you, and my **jealousy** shall depart from you. I will be quiet and be **angry** no more."

- Psalm 37:13- "The Lord **laughs** at him (the wicked), for He sees that his day is coming."

These are just a few of the scriptures that record God's emotions and how He incorporates them into His actions. And because *He* feels, His creation feels. God never wants us to deny our innate feelings, but He does want us to develop the discipline of putting them in their rightful place.

## Our Feelings are RELEVANT

Everything that God creates has a useful purpose, and our feelings are no exception (but cockroaches may be). No matter what anyone has or has not told you, no matter what challenges life has brought your way, and no matter who or what may be tempting you to think otherwise- your feelings matter! God deposited them in you for good purposes, and He wants you to recognize, comprehend, and express them for His glory!

On a physiological level, our emotions aid in our survival. Fear can stir up the adrenaline necessary for us to run from danger. Emotional attachments can foster monogamous relationships. Even babies express emotions to let us know when they have an unmet need.

Psychologically, the emotions that we express (or suppress) during childhood impact the perspectives, behaviors, relationships, successes, and failures that we adopt and encounter throughout our lives. For example, I am a first-generation North American of Nigerian descent. Like many Nigerian Americans in my generation, my upbringing did not present me with a large platform to express my emotions. Yes, my siblings and I laughed, cried, and got upset with each other. But my parents grew up in a culture that did not know how to respond to the full range of a child's emotions and, consequently, permitted only limited expressions of them. Naturally, they raised us similarly. In our house, we all knew that everyone loved each other, but you would be hard-pressed to hear the L-word in our everyday conversations.

As I went through college and then moved out on my own, I noticed a difference in how I interacted with people outside of my family. I had no problem saying "I love you" or "I miss you" to a friend, but I struggled to say those exact words to my siblings and parents. I wanted to be able to express these feelings toward them, but I was bound by what I had learned in childhood: Love did not need to be stated or felt, only known. Time and trials are slowly releasing me from this mindset, but it is an ongoing process of unlearning.

Spiritually, our feelings have a place in our relationships with God. He cares about our feelings! God is delighted when we find joy in His path for us. He hears our cries and even weeps with us, as Jesus did with Mary and Martha when their brother, Lazarus, died. We can and should bring our feelings into our conversations with God. Why hide them from Him? He already knows exactly what emotions are overtaking us before we even recognize them. If you tend to stifle your feelings when talking to God, I want to challenge you to change that today! Try this the next time you pray: Write what you are feeling. Do not worry if you do not know why you are feeling that way, just write it. Tell God in your prayer, "I feel _____. Help me understand what You want me to do with this feeling." The answer may not come automatically, but you should keep your ears, eyes, and mind open for His response. Even if there is distance between you, trust that He can and will guide you to put your feelings in their place.

God also instructs us to take others' feelings into consideration. When a fellow believer is rejoicing, we should rejoice also; and we should weep when another believer is weeping (Rom. 12:15). This scripture does not tell us that other people's emotions should dictate or supersede our own. Rather, it gives us guidance in empathy. God gives so much value to feelings that He wants you and me to be able to acknowledge and respond appropriately to the feelings of another person.

Do you feel overwhelmed by the weight of a significant responsibility, with no one to help you? Consider Hagar, cast out of the home and family she had come to know along with her teenage son. As they wandered through the wilderness, God heard the boy's voice and called out from heaven. Not only did God meet their physical needs by supplying them with water; He acknowledged Hagar's fear and despondency. God encouraged her to keep going, assuring her that her son would live and give rise to a "great nation" (Gen. 21:8-21).

Maybe you have been suffering and looking for God's comfort for some time. Consider the Hebrews, suffering as slaves in Egypt for

400 years! God told Moses that not only had He *seen* how the Hebrews had been oppressed, but He had also *heard* their crying and *knew* their sorrow (Exo. 3:7).

If you are exhausted, Jesus wants you to come to Him and find rest (Mat. 11:28-29). When Jesus said this, He did not use the Greek word *sóma (body)*, which would have indicated physical rest; he used a form of the word *psuché*. English translates this word as soul. Strong's concordance defines the soul in this context as 'the seat of affections and will.' In other words, Jesus promised that those who come to Him will find rest in the place where their emotions live. He wants to take our minds to a place of peace and tranquility. This tells me that Jesus knows what a burden our feelings can place on us. He knows that we cannot be at our best if we are constantly weighed down by very real feelings like anger, depression, or discontentment.

Now, let's be real: it can be mighty awkward to share our feelings with God. I remember listening to a man share his story about his journey to a relationship with Christ. He admitted that the idea of being intimate and "touchy-feely" with God had challenged his perception of manhood at first. He had to learn to be okay with such transparency.

I want you to know that, whether you are male or female, God wants you to be intimate with Him. Consider David- not only was he Israel's greatest king and warrior, but he was also a prolific poet and songwriter. Read the Psalms and you will find that David shamelessly shared feelings of happiness, despair, fear, anxiety, peace, and hope with the Lord. David had unwavering faith in God's ability to wipe his tears, settle his nerves, and quiet his mind. He chose to leave a legacy of emotional vulnerability with the God he passionately loved.

I believe that men, especially, should learn from David's example. Do not let the enemy deceive you into thinking that crying in front of God or telling Him how you feel makes you a weak man. This is only Satan's attempt to disconnect you from God.

## Our Feelings Should not RULE Our Actions

Here is perhaps the most important of the three R's. Even though we possess real and relevant emotions, we will not be able to have the intimacy that we desire with God if we allow them to rule our actions. God draws close to us when we allow *Him*, not our feelings, to direct us daily.

This conflicts with the world's mantra to "Do what you feel." Unless God vets and approves our feelings in the moment, it is often wiser for us to avoid doing what we feel. Of course, this does not mean that we need to wait for God's explicit approval before every single move we make. If you are welcoming someone home from a long trip, I do not expect you to stop and pray before embracing that person!

I am talking about those times when our feelings may compel us to act in a way that stands against God's word. In these cases, God's Word, whether universal or specific (Chapter 2), should drive our behaviors. Our feelings should take a backseat.

How does relying on our feelings lead us astray and keep us distant from God?

1. **We are connected to God through our spirits.** God created every part of us- spirit, soul/mind, and body. He is concerned about all three parts of us and wants us to entrust them to Him (Mark 12:30, Rom. 12:1). But a child of God connects directly to God through the spirit. This spirit is dead before we accept our salvation in Jesus Christ. But the spirits of those who believe and confess that Jesus Christ is their Lord and Savior are brought back to life and connected to the Holy Spirit (Eph. 2:1-5, Rom. 8:16). This is the part of us that always wants to please, obey, and honor God. This is not the place where our feelings dwell, but our spirits can and should rule our feelings. God wants us to open ourselves up for deposits from the Holy Spirit that will guide our feelings and actions

Do not beat yourself up if you do not do this successfully every time; nobody does. But as we grow closer to God, we develop an increasing desire to walk in the Spirit and commit to doing so more often (Gal. 5:16).

2. **Our feelings are not always rational.** Emotions are an instinctive and necessary part of us. But they are not always tied to logic or wisdom. There are PLENTY of times that I have been angry, jealous, or ashamed, but I was triggered by something that should not have evoked those emotions. Things I have gone through, lessons I have ignored, and walls I have built sometimes manifest as negative emotions towards what could have been a positive experience. Our feelings can be short-sighted, overly deductive, or just ill-fitted for the situation. We do have the ability to understand

and interpret our feelings. But this does not mean that our *feelings* have understanding. Sadness may come over me, but it cannot tell me *why* it has come over me. So, it is not always wise to let our feelings rule our actions (although it does work out well sometimes). The Bible tells us in Proverbs 3:5 not to rely even on our intellect. If we cannot trust our refined logic to give us sound direction, how much less our raw emotions?

3. **Our feelings are fickle.** Just as our feelings can sometimes be illogical, they are very often fickle. I am not a psychologist, but I am sure that any experienced one can give an estimate of the average number of emotions that one person feels in a 24-hour period. And I am willing to guess that the number is greater than five. Feelings can change by the day, hour, or minute. They can be affected by season, age, marital status, occupation, or physical ability. New information or ideas can take us from feeling afraid to relieved, nervous to confident, or proud to humbled. As our appearances, values, lifestyles, social circles, and finances change, we can be assured that our feelings will change also. The short lifespan of emotions is not a terrible thing. But it makes them an untrustworthy guide for our behavior and character. Why not look to God's word, which *never* changes? No matter how our feelings are impacted by the people and things that come and go, God's word is never affected. We can rely completely on His fixed guidance and instruction.

Why did God bother to give us feelings at all if He rarely wants us to act on them? Feelings help us communicate, empathize, and survive. We should not try to dismiss our feelings but instead recognize and reason through them. We should always take a moment to think about whether it would make the situation better or worse if we acted on them. If worse, we must set those feelings aside and let God lead our actions.

Thankfully, Jesus set the example for how this works in real life:

***Jesus and the 5,000 (Mat. 14:9-21)-*** This record follows the tragic beheading of John the Baptist. King Herod and Queen Herodias had imprisoned him for calling them out on their unlawful marriage. Eventually, they took a horrible step further and decapitated him. John's disciples told Jesus about his death. It is important to note that John the Baptist was not only Jesus' messenger and servant, but also his relative (Luke 1:36). According to Matthew, Jesus went and looked for a place to be alone after receiving the news. Although He does not explicitly state His emotions in this passage, I believe that He retreated because he was devastated by what had happened to his relative and friend. Jesus did what many of us do in the face of tragedy, so we can reason that He was deeply hurt by John's ruthless murder.

Jesus' ministry, however, was well under way by this point, and it had come with extreme popularity. Rarely did He find Himself outdoors without one or 1,000 people approaching Him. This instance was no exception. Jesus did not have long to mourn for John before a multitude of people showed up at his private place of solace.

If you are the type to draw into yourself in times of sadness, then you know how irritating it can be to have those quiet moments interrupted, even if somebody wants to comfort you. And it is downright treacherous to be interrupted by people who want you to do something for them! But this is exactly what happened to Jesus. Over 5,000 people invaded His personal space and effectively obliterated His chance to focus on His feelings.

Jesus had a choice. He could have thought about all He had done for these people up to that point and decided to continue with His (much needed) personal timeout. He could have said, "Meet Me tomorrow- same time, same place." Or He could tend to the needs of the people at once, which would require Him to set His real and relevant sorrow aside for the moment. There was nothing wrong with Jesus taking time to Himself, especially considering the reason. Similarly, there is nothing wrong with you or me taking time to be alone when dealing with heavy emotions. However, an opportunity arose to take care of God's people. Jesus had the chance to bring glory to His Father right then by teaching, healing, and feeding a multitude. If He turned them away, there was no guarantee that they would return.

Jesus chose His ministry, which was God's will for His life on Earth. Although He was undoubtedly grieving in His heart for John, He made the decision to put spiritual matters first and entrust His Father with the sadness in His soul. Because of His personal sacrifice, thousands of people received healing and food! But notice what is recorded in verse 14 *before* Jesus began to act: "…He saw a great multitude; and He was *moved with compassion* for them…" Our gracious God knew that the sorrow His Son was experiencing would not be conducive to what He needed to do for the people in front of Him. Instead, the Father allowed room in Jesus' heart for the compassion that would compel Him to care for the crowd. Jesus' sorrow was valid and justified, and He had every right to express it. But when it stood to hinder Him from seizing a God-orchestrated opportunity, Jesus rightfully put that feeling in its place. I wholeheartedly believe that God takes notice each time we set our feelings behind His will. And if we draw close and entrust our souls to the Lord, then He can make room for the emotions we need to complete whatever assignment He has for us.

***Jesus and Lazarus (John 11:1-37)***- While Jesus was in Perea, He received word that a man named Lazarus was sick. Jesus loved Lazarus and his two sisters, Mary and Martha. He had visited their home in Bethany more than once, and He considered Lazarus a friend (John 11:11).

Once Jesus received the news, he had to decide what would dictate His actions: the emotions in His soul or the faith in His spirit. Lazarus' death hurt Jesus deeply (John 11:35). And He knew that He would be hurt, just as most of us know that we will be sad when loved ones die. Because Jesus knows all things, He knew that this sickness would take Lazarus' life before he ever met Lazarus! On the other hand, Jesus also knew that it was His Father's plan to lay Lazarus down and then raise Him again. For God to get the glory out of this tragedy, Jesus would have to hold back and allow his friend to succumb to a disease from which he could have been immediately healed.

Would Jesus act to prevent Himself and Lazarus' sisters from experiencing the pain of losing a loved one? Or would He act according to what He knew was His Father's will? We should always consider Jesus' humanity. As a man on Earth, He was bombarded with temptations in all areas of His life, just as we are today (Heb. 4:15). This event presented Him with an option to follow His feelings rather than His Father. But Jesus rejected that temptation. After receiving the news of Lazarus' poor condition, Jesus chose to remain in Perea for two more days. By the time He finally made it to Bethany, his friend was dead and had been buried for four days.

On the surface, this may seem like a grocery list of failures on Jesus' part. Why was He so late? Did He make a mistake with His timing? Did He not care about Lazarus' health? Did He not care about His relationship with Mary and Martha? Why could He not have just given a word for Lazarus from Perea? There is one answer to all these questions: Jesus put His feelings in their place.

He was not engaged in a battle between life and death. To raise someone from the dead is never a challenging task for Jesus. The battle was between everyone's faith and their feelings. This applied not only to Mary and Martha, who were challenged to believe in the Lord's resurrecting power despite their grief. It also applied to Jesus, who had to act in accordance with the Father's plan despite the sorrow that He knew it would bring. Had Jesus commanded healing for Lazarus from Perea or traveled immediately to Bethany to heal him before he died, He would have separated Himself from His Father's will and robbed Him of His glory. He would have been telling God to take a backseat to His own temporary emotions.

Now I may sound dramatic, but this is what you and I do anytime that we choose to go against God's will because of our feelings. We tell God that our bodies are more sensitive to the direction of our souls than to His direction. We tell Him that when it comes down to doing what we feel versus doing what He commands, our feelings take priority. We set our current and temporary emotion, a created thing, above our Lord who created it; this is the definition of idolatry. And even if it is just for a moment, even if it results in one teeny-tiny act of rebellion, it can be a costly trade-off. If we make this our life practice, we should not be surprised when God begins to feel far away from us over time.

I know all too well what a mess my feelings leave behind when they run out of control. As I write this, I think about a time that a friend hurt me. The hurt was real and relevant. I don't know if the person knew that I was hurt, but it did not matter to me; I allowed the pain to rule my response rather than entrusting it to God. I cut that friend off without giving them another chance. This was years ago, but I still miss that friend today. I think about that time that I allowed my anger to go unchecked, and it cost me a pretty penny to fix the damage I had done. Mismanaged feelings of rejection and low self-esteem have driven me into the arms of people who never should have held me. I can think of several instances when I spoke too soon, withheld too much, or stayed too long because I had chosen to let short-sighted emotions guide me rather than the Holy Spirit.

If you can relate, then I have good news: we are in good company! Here are some Biblical examples of people who had moments of not putting their feelings in place:

***David, Nabal, and Abigail (1 Sam. 25)-*** Before David became king of Israel, he spent years traveling through the wilderness with his family and militia, fleeing from King Saul. At some point during that time, David and his men had protected the servants of a wealthy man named Nabal. 1 Samuel 25 records an incident that occurred during springtime, the season for sheep shearing.

David heard that Nabal was in full sheep-shearing (and money-making) swing. He hoped that Nabal would provide the men with food to repay them for protecting his servants. David sent his servants to the wealthy man; they warmly greeted him and humbly presented David's request. But Nabal, who is described as "harsh and evil in his doings" (25:3), was not on board. Living up to his reputation, he shamelessly refused to provide any food to the men. Adding insult to injury, he sneeringly asked, "Who is this David?" as if David's prior relationship with his shepherds had been insignificant.

David was furious when his servants told him how Nabal had treated them. It is easy to understand his anger, especially considering the society in which he had been raised. Repayment of money or kind gestures was a major tenet in the Hebrew culture, as was giving to those in need. These were principles that God honored and expected from His people (Psa. 37:21, Pro. 19:17, 1 John 3:17). For Nabal to disregard this custom was rather disrespectful, to say the least.

David was a well-known warrior at that point in his life. He revered and served the Lord passionately, but he was *not* the one to cross! Faced with Nabal's brazen dismissal, David's real and relevant feelings evoked a dangerous temptation to seek revenge. Without any recorded forethought, David planned to satisfy that temptation by resorting to what he knew well: bloodshed. He decided to let his emotions lead his actions rather than draw close to God at that moment. David and his men headed back to Nabal's home with murder on their minds. Every male in the house was about to lose his life. We read nothing about guidance from God at this point. Sometimes, He will choose to be silent when we have made up our minds to move without consulting Him first.

Thank God for Nabal's wife, Abigail, a woman praised for her "good understanding" (25:3). When she heard what had happened, she knew that David would be angry. She also feared- and rightfully so- that David would act on that emotion. She prepared plenty of food and rode out on her own to present it to David and his militia before they arrived at her home. Abigail possessed true, godly wisdom that directed her to take responsibility for her husband's foolishness, something she certainly was not obligated to do. What God chose not to say directly to David, He graciously spoke through Abigail. She warned David that if he went forward with his plan rather than allowing God to avenge him, he would be shedding blood without just cause.

David listened to this wise, brave woman and praised God for her righteous interference. We ought to praise God whenever He sends someone at just the right time to interfere with our recklessness! As David allowed himself to hear God's message, the Lord eased his temper and took away his desire to sin against Abigail's family. If we choose to let the Holy Spirit flood our spirits when our emotions are flooding our souls, then He can ease our minds and keep us from sinful thoughts, words, and actions.

***Moses at Kadesh (Numbers 20:1-13)***- Moses was a Hebrew man tasked by God to deliver his fellow Hebrews from the bonds of slavery in Egypt. The Hebrew people had witnessed God move on their behalf through Moses, displaying one supernatural wonder after another to set them free. From Moses' first encounter with the

Egyptian Pharaoh and onward, he had learned to trust God with every step as he led the mass of people to their promised land. But things changed in Kadesh.

Here, the newly freed Hebrew people complained to Moses and his brother, Aaron, because they could not find water. This, however, was not the first time they had complained. In fact, they had been criticizing Moses (and God) from the moment their feet crossed the Egyptian border. Repeatedly, for 40 years, Moses had to bear the people's ungratefulness, fear, and disobedience. So, we can certainly understand his irritation when the people came to him with yet another grievance.

Moses and Aaron asked God what to do to provide the group with water. God responded with clear, step-by-step instructions: Moses was to take the rod that symbolized his leadership, gather the people, and speak to a certain rock. God assured Moses that the rock would bring forth enough water for the people and their animals.

The two brothers called everyone together, and Moses had his rod in his hand. Everything was going according to plan. And then, Moses spoke- but not to the rock. He addressed the crowd with what came off as an exasperated and haughty tone. Leaving God out of this tongue-lashing, Moses gave the impression that *he and Aaron* were the ones providing water for the people, and begrudgingly at that. Moses then used his rod to strike the rock. Water gushed out as God had promised, and the people and livestock drank. But Moses was in trouble. He struck the rock although God had specifically instructed Him to speak to it. He acted on his frustration and pride rather than on God's word. (The command to speak to the rock instead of striking it was not some petty preference on God's part. It had significance, but that is a topic for another book.)

Despite Moses' sin, the Lord provided for the people's needs- how incredibly faithful He is to take care of His sheep when the human shepherds fail! But God handed a severe consequence to Moses for his disobedience (and to Aaron for being an accomplice). Neither of them would live to see the land that they had been leading the Israelites to for all those years. Before birth, God had called Moses to be His vessel for delivering the Israelites, and Moses indeed became just that. But he would not complete the journey with them. Just like those who had complained and doubted God's word after leaving Egypt, Moses would die in the wilderness. To be honest, this breaks my heart every time I read this passage. What a huge loss for what seems to be such a small issue! But disobedience is never small to God. Sometimes, it has grave consequences, and it always takes us out of God's manifested presence. Moses' feelings failed to direct him rightly, and they can certainly fail us as well.

## How Satan Manipulates Our Feelings

God created our feelings. Satan has no part in the creation of emotions or anything else, for that matter since he does not create. He does, however, distort, deceive, and manipulate with proficiency. And it is much easier for his lies to take hold in our minds when God is distant from us. We must protect our feelings, even when God seems far away for a brief instant or for several years. Otherwise, there are several ways that the enemy can weaponize our feelings against us and make it even harder for us to trace God.

One of his tactics could be making your feelings seem imaginary or inexplicable, attacking the **realness** of them. You may begin to wonder if you are actually feeling what you think you have been feeling. Or perhaps you may even think that your feelings are something they are not. 'Am I just feeling down, or do I have a condition?' 'Will I ever stop feeling angry, or is this just the way that I am?' 'Does God really feel far away, or am I just realizing that He has never been there?' Do not let these thoughts linger in your mind; rebuke them outright! Your emotions are real and common, but they do not define you. And God's distance certainly does not negate His existence.

Alternatively, the enemy may attack the **relevance** of your feelings by convincing you to undervalue them. This may come in the form of thoughts like *'Your feelings don't matter.' 'You will get over it.' 'You are too sensitive.' 'People really are not concerned with how you feel.' 'God is not touchy-feely; you are not supposed to talk to Him about your silly feelings.'* You may have heard this from people around you. You may even have said it to someone else. I encourage you to reject such comments from anyone and to avoid speaking them to anyone. These can plant seeds for Satan to water and cultivate into a forest of emotional emptiness. Remember that God values how you feel, and He always wants you to share your feelings with Him.

Perhaps the greatest threat concerning our feelings is letting them rule our actions and character. If Satan can convince us to *overvalue* our feelings, we are likely to be enslaved by them. Do this sound familiar? 'Well, if you feel that way, you should do something about it.' 'You have to do what feels right.' 'Act now and ask questions later.' How about this one: 'Do what's in your heart.' Unless you have permitted Christ to perform spiritual cardiac surgery on you, you cannot depend completely on your heart to guide you. We tend to give our hearts way too much credit. The world teaches us that most everyone has an inherently good heart and will generally do the right thing. The Bible, however, gives us the truth: "The human heart is deceitful above all things, and desperately wicked. Who can understand it?" (Jer. 17:9) I am not saying that our hearts will *always* steer us wrong. I *am* saying that sin has defiled and calloused our hearts. They are unpredictable and easily manipulated. Only hearts that are inhabited by the Holy Spirit can lead us wisely through life's situations.

# Reflections

1. How do I feel about God, myself, and our relationship?

2. How have my family, friends, occupation, health, or finances influenced my feelings?

3. Which truth is hardest for me to accept- that my feelings are real, that they are relevant, or that they should not rule over me? Why?

4. When was the last time I shared my feelings with God? How did I feel after sharing?

5. What role may my feelings be playing in the distance between God and me?

# CHAPTER

*Four*

## Acknowledge and Confess Sins

Before we begin this chapter, I want to warn you that it may be a difficult one. It requires us to do some deep introspection to uncover and admit things that we have done wrong. Evaluating those less-than-stellar instances of our lives is no picnic! Nevertheless, I encourage you to journey with me and take an honest look at how unconfessed sins may affect our intimacy with God. Why? Because, if we want God to draw close to us, then we must acknowledge AND confess our **sins**.

Agh. Yeesh. Did that make you squirm a little? Do not feel bad; it makes me squirm, too. Acknowledging sin is rarely in style. I do not know too many people who jump at the opportunity to admit that they have done something wrong. And when we *do* have those conversations, we may prefer to keep them superficial and lighthearted. But I believe God wants us to understand how our relationships with Him are impacted when we fail to acknowledge our sins. Although this is not the only reason that God may distance

Himself, we always benefit when we are transparent with Him about messing up.

When I am trying to find my way back to God, it helps me to remember God's position on sin and then consider practical ways to acknowledge and confess my own. Because I sin multiple times a day, I often forget or choose not to remember just how out of sync I am with God. Does this happen to you? Let us take a moment to consider the truth about God and sin.

## God and Sin do NOT mix.

Sinning against God means thinking, speaking, or acting against His standards and principles. God never has and never will commit or condone sin. This is an unchanging truth about God: He HATES sin.

God does not react to sin in the wishy-washy way that we sometimes do. He always rejects sin with His entire being. Why? Because sin is the ABSENCE of God. When we sin, we are operating independently of God; our sinful nature does not come from Him. There is no part of God that can relate to sin, and He does not teach, encourage, or force us to do it.

Now, it would be rather haughty of you or me to hate something just because we cannot relate to it. For example, I am not a huge fan of the word "baby" as a romantic expression. Weird, I know, but I usually reserve that word for folks under eighteen. I could not, however, tell someone else that they are wrong to call their significant other "baby." Just because it makes me a little squeamish does not mean I should hate it. I am not perfect; and honestly, I am just awkward with affection most of the time! But I know that other people are not doing wrong just because they are more comfortable with affection than I am.

God is neither human nor imperfect. His essence and sovereign laws are perfect in every sense of the word. So, if *He* does not like it, that means it is wrong.

God is a perfect and complete being. There is no upgrade, improvement, or sequel. This stands in contrast to the imperfect and incomplete nature of sin. It is impossible to achieve perfection through sin. In other words, no one can be perfectly evil. A sinful path eventually destroys anyone who remains on it (Mat 7:13, John 10:10, Rom 6:23). This is not just true for people. The book of Revelation promises that the devil himself will be destroyed in his sin (Rev. 19-20). On the other hand, people who live in Christ's righteousness *will* reach perfection in eternity (1 John 3:2, 1 Cor. 15:42-53).

God is also correct about all matters. Therefore, anything that we say or do outside of His standard cannot be right. If we do something differently than how Christ would do it, then we are doing it wrong. No matter how frequently or infrequently we sin; no matter how many people are directly or indirectly affected by it; no matter how much we do or do not love Jesus- sin will always be the wrong answer.

I do not want to beat a basic principle to death; but reflecting on this truth usually helps me find the light when I am stumbling in a dark place. Sometimes, I think there is some convoluted, intricate explanation when God is not close to me, when really, I am just overlooking the fundamentals. And Satan preys on my tendency to overanalyze. He is great at making things more confusing than they should be. What better issue for him to distort than the issue of sin itself? If we do not understand how diametrically opposed God is to disobedience, dishonesty, greed, and other sins, then it will be much easier to end up with blurred lines. We may find it tolerable and even necessary to dabble in sin here and there. We could misinterpret God's actions (or the lack thereof) in the Bible as Him accepting or participating in certain acts of wickedness. Then, the true God and the God with whom we identify are no longer the same. The God with whom we identify becomes more like us, arbitrarily breaking His own commandments and falling short of His own glory. I don't know about you, but that just does not work for me. I am not trying to live righteously and be gracious to people whom I would otherwise knock out for the sake of a God who messes up just like I do! I need Him to be ALL the way better than I am!

## Sin= Separation from God

As I mentioned earlier, the very essence of sin is the absence of God. When we think, speak, or act independently of Him, there is always some degree of separation.

Before Christ died and rose, the separation was eternal. God had banned everyone from heaven for eternity because everyone had sinned at least once. There was also temporary separation on Earth. God would either withdraw or remove people from His manifested presence (Gen. 3:23, 1 Sam. 16:14).

Isaiah 59 gives a sobering testimony of God separating Himself from the entire nation of Israel, a nation that He had chosen for Himself:

*"Indeed, the Lord's arm is not too weak to save, and His ear is not too deaf to hear. But your iniquities are separating you from your God, and your sins have hidden His face from you so that He does not listen" (vv. 1-2).*

*"For our transgressions have multiplied before you, and our sins testify against us. For our transgressions are with us; and we know our iniquities, transgression, and deception against the Lord, turning away from following our God, speaking oppression and revolt, conceiving and uttering lying words from the heart" (vv. 12-13).*

Other nations were threatening Israel, but God had not intervened. There might have been talk among the people that God was no longer able to save or even hear them. God's ability, however, was not the problem. His ability is *never* the problem when He does not respond as we thought He would. God is omnipotent; He can rescue anyone from anything at any time. The problem was the sins of the nation. God was *refusing* to intervene. This can occur in our lives today. God will never turn anyone who believes in Jesus Christ as Lord away (John 6:37), but He can certainly keep us from fully experiencing His presence due to sin in our lives.

This was not the first time that sin drove God to withdraw from His chosen people. Because of the wrongful actions of one man and the complicity of his family, God allowed Israel to suffer a crushing defeat in battle against the army of Ai (Jos. 7). The Israelites had just conquered the city of Jericho under God's direction, but they ended up fleeing from the battle against itty-bitty Ai after a tenth of their soldiers died. Joshua, Israel's leader, was devastated by the loss and begged God for an explanation. The Lord graciously revealed the reason for His withdrawal. Achan, one of the Israelite warriors, had taken silver, gold, and clothes from Jericho, items that God had specifically instructed the soldiers not to touch. Achan and his family paid for this sin with their lives. Only after punishment had been dealt were the Israelites able to conquer Ai.

Thankfully, those who believe in Jesus Christ as Lord and trust Him to bear the cost of their transgressions are no longer condemned to eternal separation from God. The death and resurrection of Jesus Christ guarantees a place in heaven for all who believe, but it does not allow or require God to look the other way when we fall short here on Earth. Sin was paid for, but it still brings consequences and affects our earthly relationships with God. We should never take His grace as license to continue with unrighteous habits and patterns (Rom. 6:1-2). Jesus died and rose to free us from the grip of sin. (Mat. 1:21). As Paul explained to the believers in Rome, sin no longer enslaves us once we repent and turn to Jesus Christ; we are now bonded to righteousness (Rom. 6:15-19).

## Daily Battles Against Sin

Daily battles against sin rough up the Christian journey. Temptations to think, speak, or act in ways that go against God's standard constantly bombard us. In this context, I am talking about sins that may not be habitual or premeditated. We may commit them because of circumstances, not because of our character (although I am **not** saying that circumstances justify sin). For example, panicking and lying to the boss about why we are late for work. Lingering in a conversation that includes gossip. Losing our patience in line at the store and taking our frustration out on the employees. Some people refer to such actions as small sins, harmless lies, or slip-ups; but these kinds of terms tend to downplay the severity of all sin. There is no inequality as far as sin is concerned. There is, however, a difference between committing "one-off" sins and practicing sin as a lifestyle. More on that later.

A common misconception about Christianity is that a Christian life equals a sinless life. The truth is that nobody, not even a Christian, measures up to God's glory, because everyone sins daily (Rom. 3:23). Even if we never commit another sin in life, we still would not be perfect in God's eyes because of our lineage. We are all descendants of Adam; from birth, we bear the mark of his sin (Rom. 5:12).

Contrary to popular opinion, God does not cancel us when we give in to sin. God already knew that we would never be capable of living perfect lives, so He sent His Son to live a perfect life among us and His Spirit to dwell perfectly within us. The Son's sinless life and sacrificial death served as full payment for every sin that had ever been and would ever be committed on Earth. The Holy Spirit's assignment is to sanctify those who accept Jesus' payment, making them more like Christ while living on Earth. But even Christians cannot be sinless like Christ until we get to heaven. So do not beat yourself up or walk away from your faith if you tell a lie, lose your temper, or have a moment of selfishness. Every sin is a heavy blow to God, and we should always sense the Holy Spirit's conviction when we fall short (if we do not, we may not be allowing the Holy Spirit to work freely in us). But we do not lose the battle by committing the sin. We lose when we refuse to confess and turn from that sin.

It is important for us to confess our sins as soon as we recognize them, asking God for forgiveness and committing ourselves to repentance (turning away from the sin). This is even especially essential when we cannot trace God.

If you are a believer in Christ, make time today to sit quietly, allowing the Holy Spirit to convict you gently and lovingly. Try to remain humble and open as you confess the sins that rise to the forefront of your mind- perhaps a hateful thought, hurtful word, or disobedient act. Be careful not to dismiss or rationalize anything that the Holy Spirit brings to your attention. Sincerely confess: "Yes Lord, I did (or said or thought) that, and it was wrong. Please forgive me." If you are ready to surrender to Christ as your Savior and Lord now, start by confessing that you are a sinner in need of His mercy, grace, and salvation.

Jesus will never turn down the opportunity to purify our contrite hearts and present us back to the Father, blameless and whole. God promises to be merciful to us and bring us back into fellowship with Him. Proverbs 28:13 says that those who cover up their sins will not prosper, while those who confess and repent find mercy. Confessing our sins daily reinforces weak areas in our relationships with God. No matter how trivial the sin may seem, if the Holy Spirit nudges you, confess it. You may find yourself confessing every hour of the day, and that is okay! Just know that you are not alone!

Sometimes, it is difficult for us to recognize when we have sinned. One distinguishable trait of the flesh is impulsiveness. Words and actions that we put out with little to no forethought can sometimes be the most dangerous. Our flesh thrives on quick and often ill-prepared actions. Our spirits, in contrast, direct us to be "quick to hear, slow to speak, and slow to anger" (Jam. 1:19). I am not saying that every spirit-led word or action requires a pause; moving quickly is sometimes the right thing to do. But I have discovered that checking with my spirit before speaking or acting usually gets me to a better result. Sometimes, it takes only a few seconds of pause to receive the guidance that we need.

When we do sin, Satan would rather have us overlook it. But we should be intentional about not justifying our wrongful actions. Almost 99% of the time, there *was* another option, we were *not* backed into a corner, and our hands were *not* tied. Probably 50% of the time, the other person did *not* deserve it. And in 100% of the instances when they *do* deserve it, we are free to respond with mercy and grace! God honors introspection and accountability (Psa. 32:5, Mat. 7:3-5; Rom. 12:3). If we are willing, the Holy Spirit will remind us to look at ourselves more than others and own up to our thoughts, words, and actions. But if we make a habit of brushing off the Spirit's convictions, then we will be perfect in our own eyes! 1 John 1:8 tells us that claiming to be without sin is self-deception.

On the other hand, Satan may condemn you when you give in to sin. You may think that God will not forgive you or that your sins are just part of who you are. Some people see themselves as yo-yo's, helplessly bobbing between heaven and hell every minute of their lives as they repeatedly sin and repeatedly confess. This is not the case. There is NO condemnation for those who are in Christ Jesus (Rom. 8:1)! In other words, Satan's accusations against believers in Christ amount to nothing. Before Christ, eternity in Hell was the punishment for anyone who committed any more than zero sins. But that changed when He died and rose. Now, only those who refuse to accept the sacrificial death of Christ as the full and only payment for their personal sins are truly condemned.

No amount of anything we could offer God, other than our lives, would cover the cost of even one sin (Rom. 6:23). But if you are a believer in Jesus Christ, you can rest assured that God will never look to you for payment. Your sincere, one-time proclamation of Jesus Christ as your eternal savior, not your daily confession of sin, frees you of your debt and guarantees your heavenly security with God.

What is the point of daily confession, then? Confessing our sins keeps us in fellowship with God here on Earth, because He values our honesty, humility, and dependence on Him. Although God is always with us, He is not pleased when we refuse to be honest about our sins and seek His mercy every day (Psa. 32:3-5). Intimate companionship with God is our greatest asset as we traverse the mountains and valleys of life. Do not allow unconfessed sins to take that asset away from you.

### *Sinful Lifestyles*

Sin does not come in sizes, but I do believe that there are two different "planes" of sin. We all find ourselves on the plane of falling short in our daily battles with one-off, circumstantial sins (Rom 3:23). But we can also end up on the plane of living a sinful lifestyle. In this case, one or more sins become habitual and character-defining in our lives. Lifestyle sins are practiced.

Think about two people who both graduated from medical school and completed all the requirements to become doctors. Ten years later, one of them shifts to working outside of the clinical setting. Most of her workday now consists of writing, teaching, and consulting. She does care for patients from time to time, but that is no longer her primary focus. The other still spends most of his workday in a hospital. He designs his lifestyle to accommodate his primary focus, which is patient care. Both have the doctor title, but only the second may be considered a practicing medical doctor.

Now let's go back to the two planes of sin. All who believe in Christ have the title of Sinner Saved by Grace. Some believers shift to a life that pleases God by living according to His instructions. The lifestyles that they had before no longer interest them. They still sin daily, but they are careful to confess and repent because they do not want the sin to distract them from their focus. Some believers, on the other hand, continue to live a sinful lifestyle after receiving eternal salvation. They covertly or overtly practice sin continuously and rarely, if ever, confess to God. Whether they acknowledge it or not, sin is a distinctive part of their character

Sinful habits can take root in various aspects of our lives: our hobbies, careers, relationships, the way we take leisure, or the way that we identify ourselves, to name a few. The common denominator is their effect- derailing us from God's expectations for us. These habitual sins are no different from the ones that we may commit occasionally: lying, cheating, discriminating, worrying, etc. The danger with practicing sin habitually is that it is almost impossible to maintain a healthy relationship with God at the same time. One day, we may look up and realize that we are operating completely independently of God in one or more areas of our lives.

For most of my life, I have been impatient and quick-tempered. In fact, I used to wear these traits as badges of honor. It felt quite nice to be known as the "fiery" one among my family and friends. When I did feel a twinge of guilt, I would usually try to mask my anger as passion. I thought I could control my temper all on my own...until I had a kid. Nothing else in my life to date has forced me to confront my impatience like parenthood. Do not get me wrong; I love my son, and he is a pretty mild, easygoing toddler. (That is not just Mommy goggles; other people who have been around him say the same thing, so it must be true, right??)

But being the mom of a great kid is not enough to vanquish a temper that I had allowed to run amok for decades. I can easily forget that the tasks that are second nature to me are completely new to him. I may become irritated when he takes "too long" to do something and sometimes end up just doing it myself. And when he misbehaves, I sometimes respond at a level 6 when I could have kept it at a level 3.

Through my son, the Holy Spirit was holding up a mirror for me to see the ugliness of my impatience. At first, I looked into that mirror with Vanessa lenses (My eyesight is atrocious, by the way). With my distorted, selective focus, I kept telling myself that my issues were nothing serious. But one evening, I was braiding my son's hair while stressed and frustrated about unrelated issues. As usual, he was squirming and whining, because he would much rather play than sit still for the sake of his hair. I knew this, and I thought that I could keep my temper under control. But something suddenly snapped, and all the other frustrations I had been bottling up piled on top of my irritation with his wriggling. I threw my head back and let out a blood-curdling scream. I barely recognized the sound of my voice. A part of me was shocked at myself, but I could not stop. I sat there screaming until that mirror shattered into pieces. On the other side of it was my son, literally shaking with fear. He stood there, gasping for breath and covering his ears as tears fell from his wide, terrified eyes.

Never in my life have I felt more guilty than I did at that moment. I realized that my temper would destroy my relationship with the person I love most in this world if I did not hand it over to God immediately. But as terrifying as that moment was for both of us, I am grateful for it because it forced me to acknowledge and confess my sin. Genuinely this time, with no pretense or excuses! I was in the exact place that God wanted: exposed, remorseful, and desperate for His help. He grabbed hold of me that evening and enabled me to turn away from what had become a sinful lifestyle. Finally, I stopped kidding myself and allowed the Holy Spirit to transform me. Now, when the Holy Spirit warns me that my temper is about to flare, I pause. Sometimes I breathe and count, whisper a prayer, or find a reason to laugh. I do not always get it right, but I am committed to living a transformed life.

For a long time, I had not acknowledged how deeply rooted my issues had become. Failing to address our sins can sometimes be worse than committing them. God's mercy often blocks or limits the immediate consequences of our sins. When this happens, we may persuade ourselves that all is well and misdiagnose any mitigated consequences as some unrelated mishap.

King David serves as an example. From his youth, David loved, honored, and served the Lord. God Himself called David "a man after My own heart" (Acts 13:22). As a shepherd, David trusted God to give him strength to fight off lions and bears (1 Sam. 17:34-37). As a warrior, he showed no mercy towards anyone who challenged his heavenly King (1 Sam. 17:45-51). As an enemy of the state, David sought refuge in the Lord while running for his life (Psa. 142). And as king, he established God's decrees as the nation's code of law (1

Kin 15:5). But David failed woefully in one area of his remarkable life: family.

David had a dangerous passion for women. Rather than dealing with this weakness before starting a family, he carried it into adulthood to the detriment of those he loved most. Scripture attests that David had eight wives and several concubines (1 Sam. 18:27; 2 Sam. 11:27, 15:16; 1 Chr. 3:1-4). Polygamy does not align with God's monogamous design for marriage, illustrated by Adam and Eve (Gen. 2:24, Mal. 2:13-15). David consulted God often throughout his life and kingship; but we find no record of a spiritual check-in before any of his marriages. Whether or not he realized or had planned it, David left God out of this arena.

One of the most well-known accounts of David's life is his orchestrating the murder of Uriah, a faithful soldier in his army. He wanted to hide the fact that he had impregnated Uriah's wife, Bathsheba (2 Sam. 11). When his first plan failed, David set Uriah up to be killed in battle so that he could marry Bathsheba "lawfully." Without the full context of scripture concerning David's life, this may seem like a random, although terrible, misdeed. The truth, however, is that David had been a womanizer for years and had given Satan many opportunities to prep him for this unthinkable act. David had seven wives by the time he saw Bathsheba. He had married his first wife, Michal, legitimately, and they seemed to love each other (1 Sam. 18:20; 2 Sam. 3:13-16). His second marriage might have been an effort to provide financially for the recently widowed Abigail (1 Sam. 25). Perhaps David initially justified his polygamy by assuring himself that love and provision were his only motives; we do not know for sure. But by the time he saw Bathsheba, the wickedness of this sinful practice lay on full display. David's lust and lack of self-control, the true roots of his actions, were exposed.

Sin can take the same route in our lives. We may start out justifying or rationalizing our arbitrary "slip-ups" rather than dealing with them immediately and appropriately. Eventually, these "well-intentioned" occurrences can devolve into unrighteous character traits, steadily stifling the Holy Spirit's conviction until we become immune to it.

David's entire family bore the weight of his sin against Uriah and Bathsheba. Until that point, we have no Biblical record of profound consequences against David for his polygamy. But once David took Bathsheba as his eighth wife, God had had enough. He sent a prophet, Nathan, to deliver a promise that death would overtake David's household (2 Sam. 12:10). Surely enough, calamity flooded the palace and collapsed the unstable foundation upon which David had built his family.

David's first son, Amnon, raped his half-sister, Tamar. In vengeance, Tamar's brother, Absalom, murdered Amnon. Absalom, who was David's third son, later rose against his father for the crown, forcing David to flee his palace and surrender his throne. (Although not recorded in scripture, it is believed that David's second son, Kileab, had died previously). As an affront to his father, Absalom had sex with David's concubines on the roof of the palace. And like Amnon, Absalom died by the sword (2 Sam. 13:1-18:18).

Joab was David's nephew and commander of his army. But his bloodthirsty impulses extended beyond the battlefield. With vengeance and evil ambition, Joab murdered his own cousin as well as a former enemy of David who had later formed an alliance with him (2 Sam. 3:6-38, 20:8-10). Joab was supposed to submit to David, but his lust for power expanded far past David's ability to control him.

Adonijah was David's fourth son and the one expected to take the throne since his older brothers had died. But God has chosen his younger half-brother Solomon, the son of Bathsheba, to succeed David as king. Adonijah tried to steal the crown from Solomon twice (with Joab's support). When Solomon got wind of the second challenge, he ordered his servants to kill Adonijah (1 Kin. 1:1-2:25). He also had his cousin, Joab, killed to fulfill David's dying request that he be punished (1 Kin. 2:5-6, 31-34).

Perhaps worse than the unending bloodshed was the fate of King Solomon, who followed in his father's footsteps in more ways than one. Like David, Solomon ruled over Israel and loved the Lord. Yet he, also, had no self-control when it came to women. Solomon took his father's example and ran with it, collecting wives and concubines like baseball cards. With 1,000 ladies at his beck and call, Solomon made David look like a rookie!

The tragedies of David's household were committed by adults who were each responsible for his own actions. David, however, was the one who planted a sinful seed that took root and allowed wickedness to blossom. Despite his shortcomings, we cannot deny or dismiss His love and desire for God, And God never took away His love or purpose for David. He promised that David's descendants will sit on the throne of Israel, and He continues to fulfill that promise through the eternal reign of Jesus Christ (2 Sam. 7:8-17, Mat. 1:1-17). David had a passionate relationship with God. Yet, he missed several opportunities to let God counsel him in the areas of marriage and family. David chose to navigate those courses on his own. It is easy to allow the victories in one area of our lives to eclipse the failures in another. But God wants to be involved and give us victory in EVERY aspect of our lives. If we want to keep God close to us, we must let Him into every room of our spiritual house. Any room that we lock him out of remains dark, and that darkness can seep through the entire house, turning us far away from God. David recommitted himself to God before this happened (2 Sam. 23:5), but Solomon did not (1 Kin. 11).

## False Gods and True Idols

God instructs us not to worship other (read: false) gods or create idols for ourselves. These are sins that may be difficult for us to recognize but are obvious to God. When His illuminating words shine into the dark corners of our lives, nothing can remain hidden. One of my favorite Scriptures says, *"For the word of God is living and active. Sharper than any double-edged sword, it penetrates even to dividing soul and spirit…"* (Heb. 4:12).

The one, true God can easily detect false gods that hover around our souls and stifle our spirits. If we allow these Satanic gods and idols to stay within and around us, God will not hang close. He refuses to share His glory with anyone, and He knows that we will not be able to serve two masters (Isa 42:8, Mat. 6:24). Sadly, idols and false gods have made themselves comfortable among us.

This, however, is not new. Idols and household gods pervade the Old Testament, and not just among nations that did not worship Jehovah. Israel, God's chosen people, routinely turned to idols and other gods. They worshiped Baal, Ashtoreth, Chemosh, and other false gods of surrounding nations. There were also household gods and pocket-sized, travel-friendly idols (Gen 31:19,34; Jud. 17:4-5, 1 Sam. 19:13-16).

God's people were keenly aware of His position on this matter. The first two of His Ten Commandments made this clear: No other gods and no idols (also referred to as graven images). But God's desire to be Israel's only God was well known even before they received these commandments (Exo. 32:15). Hundreds of years earlier, Jacob told his family to get rid of their household gods before building an altar to the true God (Gen. 35:2-4). The Lord's mandate never changed, despite centuries of polytheism among His people. God sent prophets like Isaiah, Ezekiel, and Zechariah to speak against the worship of false gods. And His expectation is the same for us today: Get rid of all other gods- Jehovah is the only true God!

"Little g" gods have permeated all corners of the earth, from Europe to Africa, from Asia to the Americas and beyond. How often do we examine our lives for the presence of false gods? Sounds a little dramatic, I know. But because they can creep in unnoticed, we should be on our guard, always monitoring the spirits that take residence inside of us. When we detect them, we must acknowledge their presence and confess to God that we have allowed these spirits to rule us in one way or another. Then, the Holy Spirit will help us take the necessary steps to rid ourselves of them.

Now think about any person, object, or idea that has a higher effective position in your life than God. It may be easiest to consider it like this: How would your relationship with God be impacted if you could not have a certain person, thing, or idea? If the impact would be negative, then you may have an idol in your life. Idols come in all shapes and sizes, including-

- your person (appearance, ethnicity, personality, health, etc.)
- culture and customs
- education and degrees
- titles
- material possessions
- spouse or children
- friends or significant other
- career
- church
- dreams and goals
- talents and skills
- recognition and accolades
- entertainment
- sleep
- travel
- sports
- food
- money

The list goes on. You may be thinking, so I cannot enjoy *any* of these things? I am certainly not saying that. There is nothing inherently wrong with anything that I have listed here. The problem comes if the absence of any of these would threaten our commitment to God.

Education has always been extremely important to me. At one point, however, the Holy Spirit showed me that I was idolizing it. I would judge people by their level of education, comparing it to mine to determine if and how I would interact with them. I became jealous when others around me obtained more advanced degrees. Because my sense of worth was primarily rooted in my intelligence, I felt like a complete failure when I was not accepted into medical school after college. Instead of trusting God's plan for my life, I wasted time and effort trying to pursue a career that I thought would give me influence and value. Today, I am learning to acknowledge and confess when I am feeling worthless or jealous. I am slowly embracing the beautiful truth that every person, including me, is worth more than gold simply because God created us.

Another potential idol in my life is my son. I absolutely hate to think about a life without him. But every now and then, I force myself to consider how I would respond to God if He decided to take him from me. The first time I thought about this, my answer was somewhere along the lines of "Well, God, that would likely be the end of You and me." Not the response of someone trying to live an idol-free life! Of course, I can only speculate what my response would be, and I pray that I never have to know it for certain. But I continue to examine my heart. My goal is to be able to say with all sincerity, "Lord, I would be utterly devastated and heartbroken if You took back the son You gave me. But I would still love, trust, and serve You."

Perhaps you are already living with the reality of having lost someone or something you loved, and you are struggling to come to terms with God in the aftermath. I know where you are. When my brother died suddenly at 25 years old, I was shaken to my core and thrown completely off balance. I could not understand why God chose not to prevent his death. Although I am learning to cope with the grief, it is still heart wrenching to fathom never seeing my brother's face or hearing his voice again in this life. If you have lost someone or something that you loved, do not let it ruin your relationship with God. Instead, take your broken heart to Him. Allow the God of all comfort to ease your pain (2 Cor. 1:3).

## Forgiveness

While acknowledging our sins, we also have a duty to forgive others-even if they do not acknowledge theirs! Forgiveness was a major component of the ministry of Jesus Christ and His apostles (Mat. 18:21-35, Eph. 4:32, Col 3:13, Rom. 12:17-21). He wants us to forgive those whose sins affect us. Our forgiving others should reflect the way God forgives us (Mar. 11:25-26).

Of course, this is usually easier said than done. Forgiveness can happen quickly or over time. Sometimes we must forgive people who have no remorse for their wrong. But we cannot allow the circumstances of the offense to determine if we will forgive. As sinful people, we are **all** capable of committing terrible, wicked, unthinkable acts against one another. But no offense is more powerful than our ability to forgive. That is because Satan drives sin, while God handles forgiveness. We can overcome sins committed against us because the God who gives us the ability to forgive is greater than the enemy who leads us to sin (1 John 4:4).

It is easy to justify unforgiveness or pretend we have forgiven when we have not. But God is never fooled; He knows what is in our hearts. Putting on an air of entitlement or self-righteousness opens a door for Satan to harden our hearts. He tries to convince us that we can live a healthy life and have a healthy relationship with God while unforgiveness lingers in our hearts. This is far from the truth. Unforgiveness can affect us emotionally, causing us to live in a constant state of anger, regret, or numbness. It can affect us physically with sleeplessness, headaches, weakened immune systems, high blood pressure, ulcers, and heart attacks. Most importantly, unforgiveness affects us spiritually by turning us away from God's model of forgiveness.

I have operated under the pretense of forgiveness more times than I can count. I like to convince myself that my heart is free of hate and that I am walking right next to Jesus, all the while knowing that I am holding a grudge! So, let me tell you from experience- unforgiveness is exhausting. In the daytime, the offense loops through my head like a song on repeat. At night, I will stay up thinking of ways that I want to take revenge. But for a long time, I would not acknowledge my unforgiveness; it was easier just to pretend that I had forgiven the people who had hurt me.

It was while I was going through the process of divorce that I finally came clean with God. I was infuriated with myself and so many other people, and the weight of my emotions was far too heavy for me. God instructed me to forgive myself for the foolish way I had entered marriage; my spouse for his choices and actions; and church folk for their gossip, judgments, and horrendous advice. If I chose not to forgive, He warned, then I would succumb to the darkness. My son would grow up without his mother. Most importantly, I would have lost the opportunity to let His love radiate through me.

The truth is, I cannot genuinely love anyone whom I refuse to forgive. And if I do not love others, that calls my love for God into question (1 John 4:20-21). If we do not love others, our God-given gifts become useless in His sight (1 Cor. 13:1-3). As much as we would like to believe that we are in sync with God as we harbor unforgiveness, scripture makes clear to us that this is not the case.

If you are struggling to forgive anyone in your life, go to God right now and tell Him. Admit that you need help in this area. You will be amazed at the quick response of the Holy Spirit.

Be aware, however, that Satan may emerge just as quickly to sabotage the Spirit's work. Do not be surprised if your mind immediately goes into battle, fighting between reasons to forgive and reasons to cling to the offense. Vocally rebuke the negative thoughts in Jesus's name. Focus on any thought that is giving you valid reasons to forgive; that is the Holy Spirit talking to you.

I think it is also important to understand what forgiveness is **not**. It is *not* saying what that person said or did was right. Forgiveness is *not* convincing yourself that what was done to you did not hurt you. It is *not* abandoning the physical, mental, or emotional toll that the offense took on you. Forgiveness is *not* allowing that person to continue to speak or act in that way towards you.

Forgiveness simply but powerfully says, "I choose to do for you today what God does for me every day. I separate you from what you said or did against me. I trust that God will heal any pain you brought to me. I will no longer allow your offense to interfere with my peace."

Unforgiveness tells God that we would rather deal with our pain ourselves. Instead, let us depend on God to comfort us as we commit to forgiveness.

# Reflections

1.  What is my relationship with sin? Do I fight, ignore, or embrace temptations to sin?

2.  How may sinful patterns and habits be affecting different areas of my life?

3.  How do I differentiate the Holy Spirit's conviction from Satan's condemnation?

4.  What actionable steps of repentance have I taken or will I take from the sins that I have confessed?

5.  Is my conscience clear of past sins that God has forgiven? If not, have I taken my guilt to God for help?

6.  Whom in my life have I not forgiven, and when will I begin the process of forgiving them? Why not now?

7.  What relationships can I try to restore?

# CHAPTER

*Five*

# Consider Yourself Worthy

How do you measure your worth? Life presents us with plenty of parameters to determine our value: family name, degree, career, socioeconomic status, etc. But these worldly measures never seem to provide satisfying results. How often do we fall into the "too *this*" or "not *that* enough" categories? Trying to measure worth according to the ever-changing standards of this world can drive a person mad.

Good news- God uses a different standard to determine our worth. Rough news- It is a perfect standard. Great news- He provided a way for all of us to reach it!

YOU are worthy of being a child of God. YOU are worthy of His time and attention. YOU are worthy of receiving God's miracles, blessings, and victory! Not because of who you are, but because of who our savior is. Our names, appearance, titles, money, morals, talents, and self-proclaimed good works do not have any significant value to God. It is Jesus Christ's daily intercession for us that makes us worthy! He stands before God the Father and presents us, faultless and pure (Jude 1:24). The Holy Spirit puts our attributes and skills to work for God's kingdom. Believers in Christ stand not on their own merit but on Christ's righteousness. Because of this, God is free to adopt and bless us as His sons and daughters.

## Worthy of God's Heart

God's love for us is deeper than we can understand. No matter how your relationship with God looks, He loves and cares for you. If you have ever created a product, model, or service, you may know how it feels to love what you created. God created us all and rejoices over us as reflections of His glory (Gen. 1:26, 9:6; Psa. 8:4-8; 1 Cor. 11:7). Those who believe in Jesus Christ as their savior also receive God's fatherly love. If you have children, you can probably relate to this deep kind of love.

But even these human examples pale in comparison to God's love for us. I cannot explain why God loves us so much. My mother taught me a chorus when I was young, and I still sing it today:

> *"He loves me; I cannot say why. He loves me; I cannot say why. On Calvary's cross, He suffered and bled. He loves me; I cannot say why!"*

Why and how God continues to love us when we constantly disappoint, doubt, and reject Him is beyond me. But that does not make this statement any less true: God loves you and me. He loves you no matter who you are, where you live, or what you have done.

Even if you are not sure how you feel about Him, He still loves you. If God is capable of loving people who completely detest Him (Rom.

5:8), then He can certainly love anyone who has even an inkling of desire for Him. Since you are reading this book, then I believe at least a fraction of your heart desires God. Know that He loves and desires you.

## Worthy of God's Ear

Friends often ask me to pray about different situations they are facing. Sometimes, they say something like, "I know *you* can get a prayer through!" Although it is usually just a joke, I am still slightly discouraged when I hear it. There are some people who believe in Christ but think that God does not value their prayers as much as He does the prayers of other believers. Aside from being far from the truth, this is also a very restricting belief that will keep us from receiving and experiencing all that God has for us.

Prayer is the tool that God put in place for any person on Earth to communicate with Him. He does not reject a prayer that reaches Him from a sincere, trusting, and obedient heart. God *wants* to answer prayers, and He is completely capable of doing so.

The prayers of every believer are held in golden bowls in heaven (Rev. 5:8). Believers can approach God's throne boldly and expect Him to hear and answer our prayers with mercy and grace (Heb. 4:16). We do not need a special head covering, a designated space, a human go-between, or the blood of an animal to contact God. Having some of these things may help us commit to praying regularly and increase our focus as we pray (e.g., a prayer closet or a certain song that we always sing). But God does not *require* any tangible thing to be in place before answering our prayers. The work of God the

89

Son on the cross fulfilled every prerequisite for access to God the Father. Now, all that is required is faith.

Prayer is not limited to those who have an active relationship with Jesus Christ. His death made it possible for ALL people to connect to God. The words of a popular hymn, To God be the Glory, describe Jesus' work this way: *"Who yielded His life in atonement for sin, and opened the life gate that ALL may go in."* Even before Christ came to Earth as a man, God was described as the One who hears all prayers offered to Him (Psa. 65:2). Do not think that it is impossible for God to hear *your* prayers if you have not yet given Him your life. If you have an ounce of desire to believe that Jesus Christ died and rose so that you can come to the Father just as you are, then believe it! Ask Jesus to help you with your unbelief (Mark 9:24) and confess Him to be the Lord of your life (Rom. 10:9-10). Jesus promised that He would never cast out anyone who comes to Him, for it is the Father who sends souls to Him (John 6:37).

I want to make clear, however, the distinction between <u>access</u> for all and <u>salvation</u> for all. Jesus opened the gate to the kingdom of heaven, but every individual person must make the choice to walk through. The hymn I mentioned earlier says "that all *may* go in," not that all *must* or *will* go in. God promises eternal life with Him only to those who believe and profess Jesus Christ to be the Son of God and their savior (John 3:16). Some doctrines teach that Jesus's death and resurrection mean that everyone will be saved and spend eternity with God, even if they never personally submitted to Jesus Christ as Lord. This idea of automatic or universal salvation is not true. If you have not yet accepted Christ as your Lord and are ready to do so, you can offer a prayer of surrender right now!

## Worthy of God's Hands

God does not only want to answer our prayers, but He also wants to be deeply involved with every aspect of our lives. He wants to have a say in our decisions and intervene in our circumstances. God wants to rescue, guide, and favor His children. He may hinder Himself from doing this at times because of sin in our lives (Chapter 4). And other times, He holds back to develop our character and teach us discipline. But these do not take away from the fact that God wants to be active in our lives and enable us to prosper.

No matter what you have or have not done in life, you are not out of reach. God can find you when you are lost or hiding. King David described God's intimate knowledge of his life beautifully in Psalm 139. Mistakes, regrets, missed opportunities, and even our sins do not stand in God's way unless He allows them to do so. If you believe that something in your past has excluded you from experiencing God's presence in your life today, then I hope these words give you a new outlook. God can respond to our needs in the exact way that we request. Or He can completely surprise us by intervening in unexpected ways, with or without explanation. God can even take a few steps back and be silent (hence, this book). When that happens, careful self-examination, prayer, and support from a mature fellow believer can help us understand the reason for His silence. It could be something that we have done, or it could be a test from God, as Job can testify. Whatever it is, do not lose hope! God's absence is temporary. His anger is brief, and He has no desire to withhold good things from you (Psa. 30:5, 84:11). Take a lesson from Jacob, who wrestled with an angel of God at Peniel (Gen. 32:22-32) or the Canaanite woman who pleaded for Jesus's help and would not take no for an answer (Mat. 15:21-28). Keep running to God until He answers, trusting that this is what He wants you to do.

God is sovereign and can intervene in any life as He chooses. Have you ever heard someone who has no relationship with Jesus shout His name during an emergency or personal crisis? Suddenly, help arrives from somewhere completely unexpected at just the right time! God can help anyone whenever and however He wants. But people who do not accept Jesus Christ as their Lord should never *expect* God to do any of these things for them. Those who do receive Him *can* expect God to be involved actively in their lives. Believe that you are His child and that He is a good Father.

## Why We are not Worthy

There are several reasons that we may believe we are not worthy of God's love, attention, or intervention. Our identity, skills, and talents that we lack, or regretful moments of our past can make it seem like we are shut out from the blessings and grace of God. The Bible, however, is overflowing with stories of real people whom God blessed and used in spite of their perceived unworthiness. Let us consider common obstacles that we or others place in our way, along with the stories of people who overcame these obstacles by discovering their worth to God.

### *Personal Identity*

The traits that identify us can also be what we allow to hinder us from being all God called us to be. Being a woman in a society that glorifies men. Being the youngest in a household that favors seniority. Being an immigrant in a workplace where the boss promotes only those whose names she can easily pronounce. Feeling unworthy because of our identity can be particularly tough because it is extremely difficult, if not impossible, to change our defining features. We are left to do one of three things: 1) spend our lives believing that we were born to lose; 2) undergo unnecessary and sometimes dangerous methods to change ourselves; or 3) find our identity in God. Here are three examples of people who chose the third option:

- ***Joseph*** (Gen. 37, 39-50)- Joseph was number 12 of his father's 13 children. He had neither the revered status and blessings of the oldest son, Reuben, nor the special affection and protection bestowed upon the youngest child, Benjamin. His father, Jacob, favored him because he had been born when Jacob was old; and Joseph's mother, Rachel, was the wife that Jacob had loved (as opposed to his other wife, Leah). Otherwise, there was nothing notably special about Joseph. But God saw him differently. He showed the teenager vivid dreams about people bowing before him in the future. Enduring the rebuke of his father, wickedness of his envious brothers, spiteful revenge of his master's wife, and a 13-year prison sentence, Joseph held on to his God-given worth. God eventually fulfilled His promise and elevated Joseph to second-in-command in Egypt, using him to save his family and the nation during a famine. You are worthy of manifesting the vision that God has given you. No circumstance, not even incarceration, can change your God-ordained status.

- ***Daughters of Zelophehad*** (Num. 27:1-11, 36:1-13)- Five Israelite sisters lost their father, Zelophehad, in the wilderness during Israel's journey from Egypt to Canaan. Zelophehad died without having any sons; because of custom, his daughters could not inherit his land. These five women, however, decided to appeal to the God of righteousness, knowing that He had not created them female by mistake or as punishment. They approached the leaders of Israel and demanded the rights to their father's possessions. God Himself advocated for the women. He used them to change the rule of law for women in Israel. Do not allow unjust laws and traditions to diminish your God-given worth. God will support and fight for you as you entrust your life to Him.

- *Deborah* (Jud. 1 5)- Deborah was a prophet and judge in Israel in the era before kings were appointed. In a society where men typically held leadership roles, Deborah could have rejected her gift and assignment from God, but she did not. She decided to live a life that was worthy of the calling she had received (Eph. 4:1). God used her to direct a man named Barak to defeat King Jabin, who had been oppressing the Israelites. Barak trusted Deborah's words as the words of God, and he positioned himself for battle with her at his side. After defeating King Jabin's army, Deborah and Barak offered a song of praise to God. You may consider yourself to be the underdog, but you have a significant role in God's agenda. Embrace who God has made you to be and stand tall in your calling!

### *Lack of Knowledge or Ability*

Do you feel that God has no use for you because you are not intelligent enough? Perhaps you think He does not value you because you stutter when you speak, were born with one leg shorter than the other, or lost your sight as you aged.

The truth is that you are capable of fulfilling your God-ordained purpose, no matter your IQ or physical condition. Learn from these examples of people whom God equipped despite their shortcomings.

- *Moses* (Exo. 4:10-17)- God wanted Moses to go to Egypt and deliver Israel from slavery. But when He told Moses about His plans, Moses brought up question after excuse after concern before finally coming right out and asking God to send someone else. One of his hesitations was the fact that he was "slow of speech and slow of tongue." Maybe Moses had trouble organizing his thoughts into words, or perhaps he had a physical condition that caused him to stutter or slur his words. Whatever it was, it was not an obstacle to God! He allowed Moses' brother, Aaron, to be the spokesperson; but He did not take the assignment away from Moses. Only when Moses trusted in His value to God was he able to accomplish all that God had asked him to do. God has called you to a specific purpose as well. Others may support you as you fulfill it, but God considers **you** worthy to be primarily responsible.

- *Peter and John* (Mat. 4:18-22; Acts 4:13)- Peter and John were two of Jesus's disciples during His earthly ministry. After Jesus ascended to heaven, the two men spent the rest of their lives leading people to Him by preaching, performing miracles, and organizing Christian churches. Peter and John were fishers by vocation; they did not have any formal religious education when Jesus called them. But this did not deter Jesus. He did not ask them to take any classes or sit under a mentor for a year before they could walk with Him. God gave these two men the honor of declaring the most important message of the past, present, and future. Rather than focusing on what you lack, trust God to take what you have and use it for His glory. Every good gift that we possess comes from heaven (Jam. 1:17), and Christ's power flourishes in the areas where we are weak (2 Cor. 12:9-10)

- **The Blind Men** (Mat. 20:29-33)- Jesus was on His way from Jericho to Jerusalem with a huge crowd following Him when He passed two blind men sitting on the road. They cried out to Jesus as He passed, begging for His mercy and healing touch. The crowd tried to silence the men, although they only wanted to partake in the same blessings that Jesus was offering to everyone around Him! Jesus stopped in His tracks and gave the men His attention. Like a servant before two kings, Jesus asked what the men wanted Him to do for them. Knowing that they were worthy of a miracle, the men courageously asked Jesus for sight. Jesus touched their eyes, and immediately they were both able to see. Our society today is like that crowd, ignoring or silencing the pleas of people who live with certain disabilities. No matter what you are able or unable to do, Jesus sees, hears, and cares about you.

## *Not part of the "in" crowd*

Perhaps you feel unworthy because you are an "outsider." Maybe you think you have gone too long without giving your life to Christ, and now it is not even worth trying. Or maybe you are a believer who has spent some time away from other believers. Perhaps you tried to reconnect somehow, but you did not feel welcomed. Maybe someone told you that Christianity is only for a particular group of people, a group with which you do not identify.

Remember, Jesus opened the life gate for *all* to enter. Before returning to heaven, He instructed His disciples to preach the Gospel to "all creation" (Mark 16:15) and to make disciples of "all nations" (Mat. 28:19). Although the Jewish people were the first recipients of Jesus' message while He was on Earth, He never rejected anyone based on ethnicity. And even before Christ came to Earth, God often intervened in the lives of "outsiders" to show them that they, too, were worthy.

- *Tamar* (Gen. 38)- Tamar was a Canaanite woman who married into the family of Judah, the fourth son of Jacob. Jacob's 12 sons and their wives gave birth to the people of Israel (the name God granted to Jacob). Tamar's first husband and Judah's oldest son, Er, died before the couple had any children. Er's younger brother, Onan, married Tamar according to custom, but he did not fulfill his duty to conceive a child with her who would carry on his brother's name. Instead, he used Tamar, gratifying himself by having sex with her but refusing to place his seed inside of her. After Onan died, Tamar realized that her father-in-law had deserted her by keeping his third son from marrying her. She decided to take matters into her own hands to receive the rights to which she was entitled. Although her actions were deceptive and she intentionally became pregnant by her father-in-law, God mercifully considered her worthy of His intervention. Tamar's first son was a direct ancestor of Jesus Christ. If you have ever been betrayed, rejected, or deserted, then you are a perfect candidate for God's intervention! Know and declare your rights as a child of God.

- ***The Gentile woman*** (Mat. 15:21-28; Mark 7:24-30)- Jesus had just finished healing a crowd of sick people, and He traveled to Tyre to have some time to Himself. But a woman found out that He was in town and came running to Him. Mark describes her as a Greek woman born in Syrian Phoenicia. The woman begged Jesus to save her demon-possessed daughter. But as far as the disciples were concerned, she had "outsider" status and did not qualify for any help from their master. Even Jesus appeared to reject her at first. The woman, however, counted herself and her daughter worthy of a miracle from the loving and omnipotent God. She passed Jesus' test of her faith with flying colors, humbling herself to what some may consider an insulting degree. Jesus praised the faith of this "outsider" and set her daughter free. Do not allow labels to disqualify you from God's abundant provision. You may be part of a longstanding Christian community, or you could be the only believer you know. Either way, you are not an outsider when it comes to the kingdom of God.

- **The Ethiopian eunuch** (Acts 8:26-40)- An official of the queen of Ethiopia was on his way home from worshipping in Jerusalem. Riding in his chariot, the eunuch was reading the book of Isaiah but not understanding its message. God decided that this man, who was eager to know Him, was worthy of adoption into His family. He directed Philip, a believer, straight to the eunuch. With no recorded hint of hesitation or discrimination, Philip shared the Gospel with the official and then baptized him. However much or little you know about God; He sees your willingness to learn. He will reveal Himself clearly to you.

## Past Actions

Is there anything that holds us back better than our past? I, for one, can become so wrapped up in my past that I allow it to overwhelm my present thoughts and stifle my future goals. Satan is especially fond of our previous mistakes and sins, always presenting a case against our Christ-ordained salvation, righteousness, and worth (Job 1:6-11, 2:1-5; Rev. 12:10).

The past holds dark secrets for some of us, secrets that would devastate us if they came to light. Or maybe we have already faced the consequences of our actions. How difficult it can be to grasp the amazing truth that God continually forgives us of our sins! Whatever our past holds, it cannot stand in the way of God's plans for us.

- **Isaiah** (Isaiah 6:1-8)- The Old Testament book of Isaiah records his resounding prophecies to the people of Judah and Jerusalem. Unlike other Biblical figures, we do not have a detailed account of Isaiah's life before he accepted God's call to prophesy to the nation. We can safely assume that he sinned like everyone else; but by and large, Isaiah is considered one of the "good" ones. Yet even he was forced to acknowledge his sins when He saw a clear vision of God. Isaiah feared that his filthy, sin-stained lips would condemn him. But God had different plans in mind. He forgave Isaiah and allowed him to be a messenger to God's people. Maybe you are "the good one" within your social circle. But no matter if you are a preacher, pastor, or prude, your sins are laid bare in God's presence. Nonetheless, God stands ready to forgive you and permit you to walk in your calling. You are worthy not because of *your perceived* goodness, but because of *His true* goodness

- **_The Criminal on the Cross_** (Luke 23:32-43)- Two men were condemned to death by crucifixion around the time of Jesus's trial. Luke identifies them as criminals, while Matthew specifies their crime as robbery (Mat. 27:38). The men were facing punishment for crimes that they had committed. They hung on their crosses next to Jesus, who was dying for crimes that He had *not* committed. One of the robbers joined the crowd in mocking and blaspheming Jesus. Obviously, this man was not satisfied with punishment on Earth; he was looking for a fast pass to eternal damnation! The other man, however, was keenly aware of his own guilt in the presence of the righteous Savior. He acknowledged Jesus as not only an innocent man, but also as his Lord. At that moment, a man who had robbed people on Earth sealed his future with Christ in heaven. God subjected him to an earthly punishment but saved him from the eternal one. No matter what you have done and how long you have been doing it, it is not too late for you to be rescued! All who surrender to Christ as their Lord, even if it is the last thing we do on Earth, receive the right to be called children of God (John 1:12).

- **Paul** (Acts 8:1-3, 9:1-22)- One of the most well-known Biblical figures is the apostle, Paul. He is a founding father of the early churches and a shining example of a Christian life well-lived. Before living this life, however, Paul was not just kinda-sorta on the fence about the idea of Christ as the Son of God. He was running full speed in the *opposite* direction! The first thing the Bible tells us about Paul (formerly Saul) is that he had approved the assassination of Stephen, a zealous apostle of Christ. Saul had gained a reputation for dragging Christians out of their homes and throwing them in prison. Only Jesus Himself could save Saul from his destructive path, and that is exactly what Jesus did. A remarkable conversion experience turned Saul into Paul- a resolute, unashamed, and highly gifted servant of Christ who wrote half of what became the New Testament. He boldly declared in one of his letters, "By the grace of God, I am what I am" (1 Cor. 15:10). Maybe you were once running so fiercely from God that you believe He wants nothing to do with you now. But God finds strengths in what we consider shortcomings. He will amaze you as He repurposes the energy that you spent running away from Him to empower you to love and serve Him for the rest of your life.

Satan could have had victory in the lives of all these people by making obstacles out of their gender, ethnicity, education, ability, or past actions. Maybe you have allowed him to do that in your life. Put an end to it today! Let Satan know that you are God's prized possession and that you are entitled to an intimate relationship with Him through the blood of Jesus Christ!

Unconfessed sins may put space between us and God; but they cannot propel us permanently out of His reach. The Holy Spirit convicts us immediately when we sin and lets up once we confess it. Satan, on the other hand, never stops accusing. He wants us to believe that our faults and weaknesses can shut us out of God's presence forever. God spoke clearly through Paul to shatter this lie. Neither the complexion of your skin, nor the material wealth of your family, nor the number of days you spent on the street or behind bars, "nor any other created thing shall be able to separate us from the love of God which is in Christ Jesus our Lord" (Rom. 8:38-89)!

Nobody can take this love from you. Nobody has a right to lay claim to the abundant, victorious life that God has promised you. If you are a victim of someone else's sin- be it discrimination, rape, abuse, neglect, or addiction- you are still worthy of shining in the light of God's glory! Those sinful acts against you, however unjust and traumatic, are not powerful enough to rob you of your worth. Anyone who tries to diminish your value has God to deal with. His word to Israel is the same to you: "he who touches you touches the apple of His eye" (Zec. 2:8). God is Jehovah Gibbor Milcamah, the Lord who is mighty in battle. He wants to take your case, fight for you, and win, because you are that valuable to Him. Let God win in your life today!

# Reflections

1. What have I told myself about my value to God?

2. What have others told or shown me about my value to God?

3. How can I put the parts of myself that I once considered unworthy on display for God's glory?

4. Whom may I have made to feel unworthy of God's love by my actions or inaction? How can I make things right with them?

5. What habits or relationships do I need to change or eliminate so that I can live worthy of my calling?

# CHAPTER

*Six*

# Pray and Praise

I am not a marriage counselor, but I would imagine that communication is one of the most frequently discussed topics in marriage counseling sessions. In fact, I would go as far as to say that communication should be brought up in *any* conversation that is even remotely geared toward conflict resolution. That is because understanding, intimacy, and unity are *impossible* without communication. When effective communication is lacking, we cannot fully understand one another, sustain thriving relationships, or effectively achieve team goals.

The value of communication in our interactions with each other reflects its value in our interactions with God. Communication with God happens primarily through prayer and praise. Just as people gain a better understanding of each other by talking, we understand God more as we talk with Him. And the same way that we win each other over with sincere compliments and accolades, we evoke God's affection and pleasure when we offer sincere praise to Him.

Prayer and praise, however, may be the furthest things from our minds when God feels far away from us. It may seem useless to request anything from God and downright cruel to shout about His goodness if we cannot even trace Him in our lives. But *we* widen the gap between ourselves and our creator when we refuse to bend our knees in prayer and lift our hands in praise.

## Prayer

### *If God had a Phone...*

Periodically, I scroll through the contacts in my phone to see which ones I should delete. I do this for two reasons: 1) I do not like it when things unnecessarily take up space, even on my phone. 2) I place high value on my relationships and try to narrow my contacts to people I can call without hesitation. And the nearest Chinese restaurant. Just keeping it real.

While scrolling, I usually come to a name and fondly think to myself, "Wow, I have not talked to so-and-so in a while. That's my girl/dude, though." An internal struggle unfolds between minimalism and memories. Usually, my memories win the first round. I keep the number in my phone, convincing myself that one of us will call the other soon. But when the next session comes around, minimalism wins. I delete the contact, thinking to myself, "They can always call me if they need me."

I am sure that many people can relate on some level. Most of us have those people who fall into the We-may-not-talk-every-day-but-I-still-love-them category. And that is okay! We naturally place people in our lives on different tiers of association. There is nothing wrong with having acquaintances, distant-but-cherished friends, and people you cannot go a day without talking to. And there is also nothing wrong with shifting people from one tier to another over time.

The trouble comes when we try to place our relationship with God on the wrong tier. God wants to occupy only one status through the duration of your earthly life: your closest companion. He is not okay with being an acquaintance or even a distant-but-cherished friend!

Why? Why is it not enough that we love and cherish God, that we know how to contact Him when we need Him, and that we smile fondly when He happens to cross our minds? Because God does not just want to be loved; He wants to be known. He is not satisfied with us just having direct access to Him; He wants us to utilize it! I love my distant-but-cherished friends, but I cannot tell you what they were thinking about yesterday or what their new favorite TV shows are. I love them, but I am not as close to them as I could be, because we cannot develop closeness without regular contact.

This is how it goes with God, also. There is no feasible way that we can expect to be close to God if we do not communicate with Him frequently through prayer. Daily or weekly contact may be enough to be intimate with family or friends. But closeness to God requires multiple contacts, aka prayers, every day.

If we do not truly long to be close to God, then that can seem excessive and exhausting. Unless and until our greatest desire is to know all that we can about Him, daily prayer will feel forced and ritualistic.

Thankfully, God does not have a "Delete Contact" option. Because God loves us, we always have opportunities to talk to Him. I think of the old gospel chorus, "Jesus is on the main line; tell Him what you want!" We may not relate much to main lines in the age of smartphones, but what I am getting at is this: If you pressed the call button on your phone, would God's number show up as a Recent Call or only as a contact? Would His number even be saved, or would you have to enter it manually?

Now reverse it: where do you fall within God's list of contacts? Is your number (i.e., your life) saved at all? If so, does God have to scroll through His saved contacts to get to you? Or would He find you instantly because you were talking with Him just a few minutes ago? Let us not be satisfied with the fact that He will not delete our numbers; the goal is to be a frequent caller! Foster intimacy with God by heeding Paul's words to the Thessalonian church: pray without ceasing (1 The. 5:17).

### *What Does Prayer Accomplish?*

God did not design prayer just for a daily check-in (although that is beneficial). Prayer often accomplishes what nothing else can by-

- *Presenting our case to God*-Everyone, no matter how popular or prosperous, has needs, desires, and challenges. We can try to address these ourselves by looking for worldly solutions that may or may not help, or we can hand them to God through prayer. Hebrews 4:16 encourages all believers to approach God's throne boldly, expecting to find grace and mercy in our time of need. Christ is our advocate; He wants us to bring our requests to Him in prayer (Phil 4:6).

Take Hannah, a woman from the tribe of Ephraim in Israel. She had a loving husband, but they had no children. 1 Samuel 1:5 tells us that God had closed her womb. Facing the ridicule of her husband's other wife, who had children, Hannah cried constantly. Finally, she decided to present her case to God. Although she was overcome with bitterness and anguish, she refused to let her emotions hinder her prayers. Hannah begged God for a child, and then she worshipped Him in faith. God soon blessed her with her firstborn, Samuel.

- *Aligning us with God's will*- Prayer has the capacity to bring us into alignment with God's plans and purposes. Just as a successful event must begin with uniting the minds of the event planners, God wants us to unite with Him concerning His plans for our lives and His kingdom.

This is often not easy or fun. It is much easier to pray according to what *we* want and expect God to align Himself to *our* will. But things simply do not work that way. I have faced many disappointments after praying according to my will. I have attended the funerals of people whose lives I had brought before God. I have comforted friends who were turned down for a job that I had prayed they would get. Perhaps you have experienced similar situations. We can become discouraged, bitter, or numb when life's outcomes are not what we desired. But the purpose of prayer is to discover and accept God's intentions, to declare, "Thy will be done on Earth, as it is in heaven" (Matt. 6:10). Jesus not only preached this message; He practiced it when faced with the cross (Matt 26:38-42). Although He desperately wanted His Father to provide a way out of what would be a gruesome and excruciating death, Jesus committed Himself to God's plans. And because of that, we are saved from eternal death!

When we learn to pray according to God's will, we can be assured that He hears us and grants our requests (1 John 5:14-15).

- *Positioning us to receive God's instructions, assurance, and miracles-* When we go to God in prayer, we are humbling ourselves and letting Him know we cannot address our situation on our own. We are yielding to the fact that we need Him to instruct and encourage us. God acknowledges prayers offered in humility and faith (Mark 9:23, Jam. 4:10).

The Bible documents the remarkable account of King Hezekiah (2 Kin. 20:1-11). While ruling over Judah, he became severely ill. God sent a grim message of death through Isaiah, the prophet. But Hezekiah cried and prayed, asking God to remember his devotion and loyalty. Isaiah returned to the king with a miraculous promise: God would give him another 15 years of life! Unlike Hezekiah, however, we may not get the outcome that we want. Sometimes God gives us instructions when all we are looking for is a quick miracle! But He wants us to trust that whatever outcome He brings is the best. No matter how tiny or gigantic our requests may be, the omnipotent God invites us to bring them to Him. Even if He chooses to work things out in a different way, God is always pleased by our faith.

- *Putting us in partnership with God-* A question that I hear often is, *"Why pray when God has already decided what is going to happen?"* The simpler part of a complex answer is that God wants us to partner with Him in governing the affairs of Earth. He created humankind to have dominion (Gen. 1:26). Because we are made in His image, we can exert that dominion through our words as He does.

In certain matters, our prayers activate and influence God's course of action. We then become partners with Him, acting in the authority that He bestowed upon us to influence the earth according to His will.

Joshua, an Israelite leader and warrior, partnered with God to defeat five kings who led their armies against Gibeon, an ally to Israel (Jos. 10:1-15). Joshua knew that God's will was for him to obliterate these Amorite kings, so he and the Israelite army fought valiantly. But the battle was still going as evening was approaching. In an amazing display of faith, Joshua prayed for the sun to stand still until he had destroyed the opposing armies. Even more amazing is the fact that God granted His partner's request! Scripture says the sun remained in the sky for "about a whole day." Whether this means the earth's rotation was interrupted or there was a rare eclipse, God miraculously granted His partner's request and gave victory to the Israelites!

- *Connecting us with other people-* The Bible frequently encourages believers to pray for others, the act of intercession. This makes us like Christ, who is our perpetual intercessor before our holy and sinless Father. Intercession allows us to take the focus off ourselves and empathize with someone else. It increases our compassion for others, even if we cannot fully relate to their circumstances. It is difficult to judge someone if you are sincerely and consistently praying for them. James advised believers to confess their sins to one another and pray for each other (Jam. 5:16). Pure-hearted intercession is never a waste of time. Even if the person refuses to accept help, your genuine intercession is a good work that the Father prepared you to do once you accepted Jesus Christ (Eph. 2:10). Furthermore, your prayers may be just one part of God's grand plan to change that person's life. Remember, we are partners with God. We can plant and water seeds by our prayers and actions, but God is the one who produces the harvest of a changed life (1 Cor. 3:6-9).

- *NOT manipulating or threatening God-* There are, however, some things that prayer *cannot* do. No form, frequency, or fervency of prayer can ever manipulate or intimidate God. We can never make God do something that He never intended to do. When praying, we should avoid phrases like "God, if you don't do this..." We should not pray for God to act in ways that are contrary to His word and character. Asking Him to punish someone with sickness or death, make someone's spouse fall in love with me, or bless me in a position that I acquired through ungodly means is a sign that I either do not know or do not care about God's nature. This takes me back to my preteen years, when I was into video games. Nothing would vex me more than my character (or avatar, or whatever you call them) jumping from a cliff or giant mushroom and not making it to the other side!

Watching them fall repeatedly into the deep abyss would bring legitimate tears to my screen-fried eyes. Being the kid that I was, I would bring God into my predicament as I approached my last chance to clear the jump. With gritted teeth and shaking hands, I would whisper, "God, if you don't let me get to the other side, I'm gonna stop worshipping you." Then I would press the jump button on the console like my life depended on it! Of course, the character would sink into the blackness for the last time, and those dreadful words would appear: "Game Over." I would open my reckless mouth and say, "Okay God, I'm done believing in You." Obviously, I thought He was my genie! Thankfully, my foolishness usually lasted only about five minutes. I am even more grateful for God's patience and mercy to me!

That may be a trivial example, but we can find ourselves in risky or even life-threatening situations when we try to manipulate God. He has convicted me of offering prayers that were way more sinister than those video game ultimatums. More than once, I have made requests for God to perform witchcraft against people I considered enemies. Graciously, God chooses to warn me rather than hand me the punishment I deserve!

When Jesus was on Earth, Satan tempted Him to put His mortal life in danger and strong-arm God into saving it. Rather than listening to Satan, Jesus repeated Moses' command to the Israelites: Do not test God (Deu. 6:16, Mat. 4:7).

## *How to Pray*

Maybe you are not familiar with prayer and are afraid of getting it "wrong." Or maybe you were once committed to frequent prayer, but a major life event disoriented you and caused you to question its effectiveness.

The most important thing to know is that we are off to a good start any time that we talk to God. The job of the Holy Spirit is to guide our prayers and speak for us when we do not know what to say (Rom. 8:26-27).

Jesus, however, left us with a model for prayer (Mat. 6:9-13). Based on this, our communication with God should express:

- proper recognition and adoration of God (v. 9)

- submission to God's will over ours (v. 10)

- dependence on His sustenance (v.11)

- a plea for forgiveness and commitment to forgive (v. 12)

- a request for protection from evil and power to resist it (v. 13).

Our prayers may go beyond these points, and some prayers may not hit each one. But having this model, we cannot use the excuse of not knowing how to pray. We can whisper, shout, stand still, pace, laugh, cry, lift or clasp our hands, open or shut our eyes. However we pray, and whatever we pray about, we should do it with faith and sincerity (Matt. 6:6-8; Jam. 1:6-7).

There is nothing too big or small to take to God in prayer. He wants us to discuss every area of our lives with Him. This is not some tyrannical command to seek His permission for our every move. God is looking for intimacy, which grows with frequent conversations. He waits for our questions, concerns, and random updates! If we need something done, He wants us to trust that He will either do it Himself or enable us to do it. Many of life's challenges do not end with prayer alone; they must be accompanied by action. But we should not try to face any challenge without *starting* in prayer. Pray at all times in the Spirit (Eph. 6:18). Pray in faith, knowing that the fervent prayers of the righteous are powerful and effective (Jam. 5:16).

## Praise

If you have any person in your life other than yourself, chances are you have wanted that person to do something for you at one time or another. Perhaps you have tried different methods to get them on board and have gotten different results. Would you agree that one of the best ways to get someone to do something for you is to praise them for what they have already done? Most people like to know that they are appreciated and that their efforts are recognized.

This universal human trait is by design; our creator also loves praise. And unlike us, who often seek unmerited praise, God always deserves it! Honestly, we cannot even offer Him the amount and quality of praise that He truly deserves. If we wanted to model the perfect praise that God receives in heaven, we would have to be completely sinless and forgo essential human activities like sleeping and eating. John, a disciple of Jesus, received a revelation of heaven and testified that praise never stops there (Rev. 4:8). All the languages in the world combined do not have enough words to express God's character and perfection. There is not enough time to praise God for every singular action that He carries out, although each one is praiseworthy.

We should not, however, allow these limitations to discourage us, because our perfect God loves our imperfect praise! When there is distance between us and God, our praise can reunite our hearts with His.

God commands our praise, as we can see in the Scriptures. But why is praise so important to Him? Is He that desperate for recognition? Would He rather we simply ignore all the challenges, emotions, and pain that we are facing to rave about how great He is, just for His enjoyment? And how can He force us to praise Him when He does not seem to be around?

The true purpose of praise goes much deeper than pleasing Him with kind words. He requires us to praise Him because He wants to equip us with the most effective tool in this spiritual war between good and evil. Satan tries to frame God as a narcissist who is concerned only with the glory of His name, unbothered by the problems we face here on Earth. The truth, however, is that God is keenly aware of every challenge that arises throughout our lives. He wants us to look to Him for help rather than trying to overcome them on our own. And the only way for us to look at Him continually is to praise Him continually. Praise is a God-given strategy for us to focus not on our troubles, but on the only One who can give us true victory from those troubles.

## What does Praise Accomplish?

Praise brings pleasure to God, but it also does many things for us:

- *Shows recognition of God's essence and appreciation for His works-* When we praise God, we tell Him, "I know and love who You are. I recognize that You have done what no one else can do." Whether in song, dance, or writing, praise reveals our thoughts about our creator and Lord. God wants us to know Him, and genuine praise confirms that knowing Him is also our desire. It is important that our praise focuses not only on God's works, but also on who He is. This takes us back to chapter 1: recognizing the beautiful, all-powerful, incomparable God for who He is. Praising God for His nature strengthens our relationship with Him because He knows that we are not only after what He can do for us. After dedicating the son of her prayers to God, Hannah sang a song that recognized God's unique nature as well as His incredible deeds (1 Sam 2:10).

- *Uplifts and encourages us-* When we are feeling down, we may want to distract our minds and temporarily block that feeling. We have several options: TV, food and drinks, friends, sports, or retail to name a few. All these options are enjoyable, and they may take our minds to a happier place for a moment. But we cannot rely solely on any of these to put whatever is getting us down in the proper perspective. Only praising and worshiping God can truly do that, because God is the only source of pure, unconditional joy. Focusing on Him fills our hearts with incredible joy and causes us to see things from a different perspective. I cannot fully explain this supernatural phenomenon; I can only suggest that praise feeds the spirit. When your spirit is fed, it becomes stronger than your feelings (chapter 3). Your indwelling spirit knows and rests in the fact that God is in control of every situation on and beyond the earth. With such a vast scope of control, He can certainly take care of whatever weighs us down! The chorus of one of my favorite hymns says this: *"Turn your eyes upon Jesus. Look full in His wonderful face. And the things of Earth will grow strangely dim in the light of His glory and grace."* Take an example from David. He often had to turn his eyes away from the world and look fully to God to compose the beautiful lyrics recorded in the book of Psalms.

- *Gives us ammunition against our enemy-* Genuine, unhindered praise is a powerful weapon as we stand in battle against the powers of darkness. One of Satan's tricks is to make you think that he is at war against *you,* and you must fight on your own. The truth is that Satan declared war against *God* when he tried to defy Him in heaven, and he has been fighting God ever since. Satan already knows that he will lose in the end, but he wants to drag you and me down with him as casualties. Our mortal minds and bodies are no match for him; but our praise invites God, who is the true opponent, into the ring. Our praise should be humble and sincere, which stands in contrast to the prideful, insincere praise that Satan (Lucifer) offered to the Lord in heaven.

Praise as a weapon of warfare is illustrated several times in the Old Testament. Israel was a relatively small nation, but its soldiers were valiant. Several battles were won by the strength and prowess that God gave them to rip through the opposing army. But in some battles, praise was the primary tactic; fighting played a secondary role or no role at all. Praise brought down the walls of Jericho so that Joshua could lead the Israelite soldiers in to take the city (Jos. 5:13-6:21). King Jehoshaphat defeated the Ammonite and Moabite armies after he and the Levites offered praise to God (2 Chr. 20:21-25). David likened praise to a double-edged sword to use against enemies (Psa. 149:6-9).

- *Keeps us humble and close to God when things are going well-* So far, we have focused on the importance of praise during tough times. But it is just as important to praise God when things are going well (Jam. 5.16)! When we meet our goals and are "living the dream," we cannot forget to give God all the credit (Deu. 6:10-12, Psa. 30:1-3). Ideal circumstances are never the result of good luck. Sometimes, they are the result of our ability and hard work- but only partially so. Say someone puts all their effort and brainpower into a project for months. Unbeknownst to them, the day that they plan to present the completed project is also the day that God has appointed for them to die. No degree of human effort or intelligence can change that. So, whatever good we can accomplish or experience on Earth is ultimately to God's credit, because He has chosen to give us another day to live.

Praising God draws us close to Him, which in turn draws Him close to us (Jam. 4:8). The strongest love is the one that is not contingent on favorable deeds. This is why a parent's love, when expressed in a godly way, is unlike any other human love that a child will experience.

God is the same way. He loves us no matter what we do for Him, and He wants us to love Him in the same way. Noah (Gen. 6:9-10:32) and Job (Job 1-42) can testify that exalting God in good times equips us to trust Him in bad times.

## How to Praise

God is always pleased with sincere praise from a heart that adores Him, no matter how that praise looks or sounds (Psa. 149:1-4). He does, however, give us some guidance in this area. Effective praise-

- is demonstrative (2 Sam. 6:15-16, 21-22; Psa. 47:1, 150:3-5).

- is public but should also happen in private (Psa. 18:49, 35:18, 119:62).

- is continuous (Psa. 34:1).

- is for God alone (Dan. 3:18).

- should not come from a mouth that curses others (Jam. 3:9-10).

As you are seeking God, be intentional about praying and praising. Even if you do not hear immediate answers, know that God hears every prayer (Psa. 65:1). If you have lost everything but the air in your lungs, He is worthy of praise even for that! (Job 1:21)

## Reflections

1.  What life experiences, if any, might have kept me from praising or praying to God at any point? How did I feel when I was not communicating with Him?

2.  Do I genuinely believe that God is worthy of praise and receptive to prayer? If not, why not?

3.  Whom can I trust to pray for me while I gain or regain the strength to pray for myself?

4.  What thoughts or activities put me in the mood to praise God? How can I incorporate these into my daily routine?

# CHAPTER
## *Seven*

# Trust and Wait

There is a popular hymn that says, "'Tis so sweet to trust in Jesus..." But I would like to propose a keeping-it-real remix: 'Tis so TOUGH to trust in Jesus! Let's be honest- it is not always easy to trust that God is working things out for us. Add waiting to the equation, and it just feels like cruel and unusual punishment. Why? Probably not because there is a chance that God will fail to deliver, but because both trusting and waiting require us to release control. Some people are naturally laidback and able to go with the flow, so not being in control may not be the end of the world for them. And then there is *my* kind of people. We like to believe that we are solely responsible for the order and structure in our lives. For us, relinquishing control is not too different from riding the tallest roller coaster in the park without a harness.

I think, however, that personality is only partially responsible for how well we can surrender control. Trusting and waiting are difficult, to some degree, for everyone, because everyone was affected by the sin of Adam (Rom. 1:19). When he and his wife ate from the tree of the knowledge of good and evil, they did more than enjoy a piece of forbidden fruit. They made knowledge an idol for themselves and all humanity. To be clear, I am not saying that knowledge is a wicked thing. God created us as thinking creatures. He endowed us with brains that are superior to every other creature because He wants us to have dominion on Earth. He wants us to be curious and studious (Pro 4:7, Ecc. 7:12, Hos. 4:6).

But God never intended for us to be so hungry for knowledge that we would turn away from Him to acquire it. Yet, that is exactly what Adam and Eve did when they listened to Satan and ate that fruit. Now, all humanity wrestles with the temptation to know what God has not chosen to reveal. Trust, which demands that we be satisfied with *not* knowing what God has not yet revealed, is against our fleshly nature. But thank God that we are not just hunks of rebellious flesh; we are spiritual beings, made in His image. And each of our spirits desires to trust and wait on God humbly and wholly!

So how can we get past our unwilling flesh and give God the control that He desires? Well, God already *has* all the control. But He has been known to back up and allow those of us who demand control to strut around for a while, thinking that we have it. If you have a child, you have likely done something similar at one point or another. But we do not want to land in a place where God says, "Okay, *you* take the reins." When we push Him to that point, we are pushing Him away. Some people flat-out refuse to surrender control to God, altogether rejecting His revelation, salvation, and instruction. Tragically, God gives these people over to their evil desires (Rom. 1:18-32). If you believe in Jesus Christ as Lord, then God will never permanently separate Himself from you. But even a slight rift can bring massive consequences. Satan's plans against us have a greater chance of success when we are not intricately connected to God. Exercising our faith by trusting completely and waiting actively on God helps us stay close to Him.

## Trust

Is it hard for you to trust that God is aware of a trial you are currently facing? Or does your relationship with Him feel off and have you doubting that He is always with you? Whether it is God's aid or affection that is in question, we can look to Proverbs 3:5-6 as a guide to trusting Him:

- "...*with all your heart* (mind)..."- True intimacy with God relies on our wholehearted trust in His love and plans for us. God knows when our minds are only somewhat committed to His agenda. The danger in this is the potential for the devil to seize that portion of the mind that is uncommitted. He will take whatever amount of our trust he can get, because partial trust in God often yields partial obedience to God. We may think God is satisfied when we operate in partial obedience, but He considers it total disobedience (Jam. 2:10).

- "...*and lean not on your own understanding*"- The opposite of trusting God wholeheartedly is leaning to our understanding. David is not saying that we should reject secular education and throw away all that we know about the world when we give our lives to Christ. But when we face problems, especially spiritually rooted ones, we should not allow our limited, worldly wisdom to have the final say about the solution. Again, the devil wants possession of even a fragment of our trust. But this does not have to sound like "I trust the devil." Turning to our own understanding, or any source of "wisdom" other than God's, is a win for Satan. Eve did not eat the forbidden fruit until *her* understanding convinced her that it would be beneficial to her (Gen. 3:6).

- *"In all your ways, acknowledge Him…"*- Our goal should be getting to the point at which we regularly invite God to the table concerning each of our actions and thoughts. David encourages us not to entertain ideas or take intentional steps that do not include God. Instead, we should seek, recognize, and appreciate God's wisdom as often as necessary.

- *"…and He will direct your paths"*- As we commit ourselves to these actions, we can expect God to give us clarity. We should expect to see, hear, and feel more frequent signs of His presence and instruction. God will never back away from the opportunity to lead a heart that looks earnestly to Him alone for direction. David, who experienced victories on the battlefield and in his personal life, proclaimed that "Some trust in horses, others in chariots, but we trust in the name of the Lord our God" (Psa. 20:7).

Trusting God is spiritual exercise. We do not work *for* our salvation, but we must work it out once we receive it (Phil 2:12). Think of this like your muscles. You did not work to get your muscle cells; they came included by right of your existence as a human. But throughout your life, you must work those muscles out if you want to get any effective use out of them.

But how do we work out faith?

First, we must believe and proclaim His word as it applies to our current situation. It may be a message that we find in the scriptures or one that God once speaks directly to us. Whether a written or spoken word, it is powerful, relevant, and intended to be fulfilled. Notice that there are two things to do here: believe AND proclaim. These actions go hand-in-hand throughout our Christian journey (Mar. 9:23-24; Rom 10:9-10). It is not enough to do one without the other. Belief is barren without proclamation, and proclamation is pretentious without belief. So go back to the Bible. Think back over your past conversations with God. Recall any prophetic message that was rightfully and responsibly spoken concerning your life. And make the decision to believe and proclaim the words to be true.

Once you begin to do this, expect Satan to defend what he is trying to hold hostage from you, whether it is your intimacy with God or a promise that God made to you. He will throw fiery darts at you that may take different forms. It is our shield of faith- believing, proclaiming, and acting on God's word- that will extinguish those darts (Eph 6:16).

Keep your shield in place by ridding yourself of complaints and internal negativity. What do we tell ourselves that runs contrary to what we want from God? What complaints do we have against Him? Revisit some of the previous chapters in this book if needed to remember what is true about God and about yourself. Learn to recognize the difference between sober introspection that is guided by the Holy Spirit (Rom. 12:3) and destructive self-criticism that is fueled by Satan (Rev. 12:10). When temptations to talk down to yourself or grumble against God arise, stop them in their tracks-rebuke them aloud if you must! Command your mind to redirect your thoughts to God's word (2 Cor. 10:5). No matter how close the disaster is or how far away God seems to be, remind yourself that He will not fail you. Make the declaration of Job your anthem: "Though He slay me, yet will I trust Him" (Job 13:15).

Along with internal criticism, there may be naysayers within your circle. They may be people who are not particularly fond of you or people who love you dearly. Even our loved ones can give us messages that do not align with what God has told us.

We can change the messages that we give ourselves, but we cannot do this for anybody else. Having a conversation with someone who speaks negatively to you may help, but the decision to modify their speech rests with them. You do, however, have a right to separate yourself. Create a barrier between yourself and anyone who continues to speak against that for which you are trusting in God.

This barrier does not have to be physical; you can live in the same house with the person and still guard your mind against their negativity. The barrier also does not have to be permanent. And if the issue is with a loved one, then I hope the barrier does *not* become permanent. I hope that your relationship will be restored and even stronger in time. For now, the barrier is necessary. No human relationship is worth losing your trust in God's word and plan.

Jesus set the example when Jairus, a leader of the Jewish synagogue, asked Jesus to heal his sick daughter (Mark 5:21-24, 35-43). By the time Jesus (and the crowd) got to Jairus' house, the young girl seemed to have died. But Jesus made a declaration: She was not dead, only asleep. This got a lot of laughs from the people inside the house. But

Jesus was concerned with the faith of only one person- the man who had sought Him for healing. He only told Jairus to believe Him. Jesus did not waste the moment trying to convince bystanders that His word was powerful and guaranteed. Instead, He simply "put them all out!"

Now, before you start hitting that Delete or Unfollow button, pay attention to this: Not every critique is equivalent to naysaying. Just as it is important to distinguish self-examination from self-condemnation, we also need to be able to tell the difference between unhelpful opinions and sound advice. God often uses people in our lives to give us the truth that we need to hear, no matter how tough it may be. The advice of a trusted confidant with an outside perspective or the recommendations of an acquaintance with a similar experience can keep us from wasting time and effort or suffering pain. How can we know what to heed and what to reject? Legitimate, God-sent advice always ultimately aligns with the word He gave you. If you are unsure, take the advice to God and ask Him how you should respond to it.

Trusting God is a surrender of the mind, a result of hearing and believing God's Word (Rom. 10:17). It is internal: your spirit assures your soul that it can trust what God is telling you. Waiting deals with our external response to our trust.

## Wait

Can you think of three people you personally know who enjoy waiting? When was the last time you said to yourself, "I am so excited to stand in this line!"? Nobody naturally enjoys waiting. Some people may tolerate it better than others, but to find actual pleasure in waiting requires an intentional rejection of our intrinsic inclination for immediate gratification. It requires discipline, faith, and proper perspective. Waiting requires God, and God requires waiting! No Christian journey- no human journey, really- is complete without waiting. Since we must all wait at one point or another, we may as well learn to do it effectively!

Just for fun, count how many times the word "wait" appears in the Bible. Of course, this will vary depending on the version or language of the Bible that you are using. But expect to see at least 120 occurrences of "wait" or a closely related word. Any verb that appears that often deserves our attention because its frequency is not a coincidence. We must wait on people and God throughout our lives because God has designed life on Earth to be this way. He engineered the act of waiting to produce a glorious side effect, whether you are waiting for ten minutes or ten years: greater dependence upon and closeness to Him. The Holy Spirit wants to renew our minds so we can focus on this outcome rather than on the burden of waiting.

Knowing how essential and productive waiting is, how do we do it effectively? How can we win while waiting? Let us go back to those three essentials for waiting: **faith** to obey, **discipline** to endure, and **proper perspective** to enjoy.

## *Faith*

Contrary to what some may think, waiting on God usually requires action. And winning while waiting requires obedient action. Faith and obedience are two sides of the same coin: we need some degree of faith to obey, which in turn produces greater faith. Without faith, which is connected to obedience, we cannot please God (Heb. 11:6).

Our faith is so important to God that He routinely tests it for authenticity and breadth. God wants to know (rather, He wants *us* to know) if our faith is real. Do we honestly believe, accept, and love Him? Or do we follow Him just to avoid Hell or to fit in with other people? If our faith is indeed real, how broad is it? Does it cover God's existence, sovereignty, perfection, infallibility, love, nearness, omniscience, wrath, grace, and eternal victory? Or do we embrace some truths about Him while rejecting others?

Perhaps you have taken Gary Chapman's Love Languages test. The goal of this test is to determine which of five external actions most clearly translates to you as love. Well, we do not need to test God to figure out His love language, because He has already revealed it: obedience! Jesus stated this plainly to humanity: "Whoever has and keeps My commands is the one who loves Me" (John 14:21). God translated David's devout obedience as love: "I have found David…to be a man after My own heart, who will carry out all My will" (Acts 13:22). Obedience- not catchy songs, riveting sermons, or Christ-centered merchandise- is the most effective way to win God's affection and bring Him near to us.

I know what you are thinking: *How do I know what to obey if God is not saying anything to me? That is the whole reason I picked up this book!* I hear you. Remaining active while waiting can be tricky because sometimes we struggle to figure out what the right thing to do is, if anything at all. But you likely know more than you think. What was the last specific command that you remember receiving from God? If you do not remember or do not believe you have ever received one, you still have His written word laid out in the Bible! When you cannot figure out what to do, do what you find there.

Whatever you do, do all that God instructs and nothing less. If the last instruction that you remember from Him was to relocate from the east to west coast of the United States, then do not stop short somewhere in the Midwest. If you are an employer who had to lay off 75% of your employees due to an unforeseen crisis, take care of the 25%. If you have had dreams of speaking in front of thousands of people but have only your family to hear your message right now, speak to them. God often looks for faithful obedience in what we consider "small" matters before assigning greater tasks to us (Matt. 25:23).

Do all that God instructs and nothing more. We can go above and beyond the expectations of a parent, teacher, or boss by doing more than they asked us to do. This is not the case with God. His instructions are perfect and already designed to be "above and beyond" expectations (Matt. 5:38-42). Anything extra is disobedience, and it takes faith not to add our own strategies to God's plan.

Let us look at Rahab, a Canaanite woman living in Jericho at the time of its impending invasion by Joshua and the Israelites. Rahab's faith in Israel's God compelled her to help the spies that Joshua had sent to survey the city. Before leaving, the spies gave her specific instructions that would save her and her family. She needed to bring her family into her house and tie a scarlet rope to her window… That was it. I don't know about you, but I would need a teensy-weensy bit more assurance than some red string if I knew that an army was coming to take over my city! Rahab could have taken extra precautionary measures to protect her home and family. She could have tried to convince friends and neighbors to come into her house for safety. Or she could have surrendered to the siege and done nothing to protect her family. But we have no record of Rahab doing anything other than what the spies had instructed her to do.

You know that you are waiting in faith if you are not looking for other solutions to give you what you want or need. In this age of immediate gratification, where there is an app or guru for just about everything, saying no to quick fixes or cheat codes can be extremely tough. But godly faith grants us tunnel vision that zeroes in on God's commands and turns us away from any alternative.

Saul was Israel's first king, but his reign was cut short due to his disobedience. He presented a burnt offering to God without permission; this was the job of Samuel, the prophet and judge over Israel. Saul claimed that he had no choice and was seeking God's favor, but God saw through his false piety. Lack of faith in God's timing pushed him to act with pride and impatience; for this, God promised to remove the kingship from his hands (1 Sam. 13:1-14).

Godly faith strengthens our spirits, conditions our minds, and subdues our flesh so that we can please God by our obedience. Show God that you love Him by obeying whatever you know He has instructed you to do.

## *Discipline*

God demonstrated repeatedly throughout scripture that He prefers to test our faith through trials, particularly trials that force us to wait. Trials have an incredible knack for *weeding* out false faith and *working* out true faith. We cannot work *for* faith, but we should work *by* faith once we receive it by hearing God's word (Rom. 10:17, Jam. 2:17). Good works are the output, not the input, of salvation.

To produce quality work, we need discipline to endure.

One of the laws of physics is work= force x distance. Is it surprising that this earthly principle reflects a spiritual one? **Good** work= *faith* x *discipline*. The greater our faith, and the longer it endures through discipline, the more often the Holy Spirit can bring good works out of us. The writer of Hebrews tells us that endurance is necessary to do God's will and receive His promise (Heb. 10:36). On the other hand, Paul warns us that even believers in Jesus Christ can produce shallow, low-quality work that will not withstand God's litmus test (1 Cor. 3:13-15).

Think about the Olympics. Perhaps every athlete who is at least somewhat serious about his or her sport imagines at some point what it would be like to compete on the Olympic stage. A sizable number of those daydreamers are likely to go one step further by gathering information; they may look on the internet or talk to coaches and fellow athletes who have participated.

While most of the information gatherers may go no further than that, a fraction of them decide that they want to compete in the Olympics. Some stop right there with the decision. Others begin to train and condition. As the intensity of the preparation increases, however, commitment wanes for some of the athletes. Gradually, they begin to fall off, patting themselves on the back for putting in the effort.

A small percentage of them, however, makes it through the rigorous training and conditioning. With heads high and adrenaline pumping, they smile and wave to the cheering crowd during the opening ceremony of the Olympic games. Then the testing begins.

Round after round, the quality of each athlete's preparation is exposed. Each test leaves an increasing number of competitors behind. Their accomplishments are remarkable, and they can return home with the exciting story of having competed in the Olympics.

A tiny portion of the athletes, however, is not satisfied with just imagining, researching, deciding, training, waving, or even competing. Their goal is to win, period. Somehow, they pass every test. They may see fellow teammates leave the field in defeat, but that does not deter them. They may suffer injury or under-perform at several points along the way, but that does not discourage them. It becomes clear that no test can overcome their will and training. These are the athletes who stand with tears in their eyes and hands raised in victory as gold medals are laid around their necks. They have won the ultimate prize. More importantly, their character and endurance were strengthened throughout the challenging journey.

We can consider the journey of our lives in the same way. Accepting Jesus Christ as Lord and Savior is the decision, Christian life on Earth is the Olympics, and a heavenly reward is the gold medal. Some people never even consider reaching for that medal. Some gather information about it, and others decide to commit themselves to Christ. Of these believers, some are content with the guarantee of eternal salvation. Others begin their Christian journey on fire but simmer down at one point or another. Some reach a certain point, look around, and decide that they have done enough for God.

All believers have eternal salvation, which is the blessed miracle of God's redemptive plan. But He is looking for people who want more. God wants us to have enduring discipline that will give Him license to do ALL that He has planned to accomplish through us. He needs people who commit every day to fighting a good fight and finishing the race (2 Tim. 4:7). So, He presents us with trials of all kinds, sometimes making it almost impossible to trace Him. He wants us to do more than conquer the challenge; He wants to develop our character along the way. Each trial has the potential to make us stronger, wiser, and more mature (James 1:3-4).

If you are going through a challenging time and not feeling God's active presence in your life, let discipline carry you through. Pray to Him as if He is near. Thank Him as if He has already answered your request. Praise Him as if He has already rescued you from your trial. You may not understand this difficult moment that you are facing, and you may not feel like praying, praising, or giving thanks. That is okay; do it anyway.

## Perspective

One of my favorite TV shows is "I Survived," which narrates true stories of people who overcame life-or-death situations. Some recount the terrifying details of an armed robbery, while others recall being stranded under an avalanche of snow for days. They vary by age, location, and experience; but there is one thing that most of them have in common. They may phrase it in different ways, but my brain processes it all the same: the proper perspective. Forcing their minds to think like survivors is the key factor that kept many of these people from giving up their fight. Some chose to focus on loved ones, some reminded themselves that things could be worse, and some learned how to get into the minds of their attacker. Whatever the strategy, they changed their perspective to survive.

God wants us to approach each day of our lives with the right perspective. He commands us to praise Him because it shifts our focus from our temporary troubles to His perfect purpose (chapter 6). Maintaining a godly outlook on everyday life makes it much easier to see our trials from God's point of view. We can think like survivors, even when everything and everyone around us seem to be passing away. We can choose to be grateful for what we have in times of need. We can focus on God's love for us when nobody else seems to care.

We win when we find joy in waiting. Satan's goal is to depict waiting as an agonizing and unfair punishment from a God who enjoys seeing us suffer. But we must reject the temptation to think this way because it is not the truth. God knows how difficult waiting can be, which is why He encourages us to look to Him. He wants to accompany us to the destination, building Christlike character in us along the way.

Rather than believing Satan's lies, recite the words of Lamentations 3:25-26: "The Lord is good to those who wait for Him…It is good to wait quietly for the salvation of the Lord." David began Psalm 43 pleading for God's rescue and vindication; yet by the end, he was commanding his soul to hope in God and not to be discouraged (Psa. 43:1-5). Sometimes, waiting is painful. Paul, who endured imprisonment, stoning, shipwreck, snake bites, and house arrest, was so convinced of God's purpose that he took glory in his suffering (Rom. 5:2-4).

Perhaps the easiest way to gain the *wrong* perspective when waiting on God is to compare your life to that of someone else. The problem with this is that everyone else's life looks great when we are the ones waiting and suffering! Watching people succeed while living deliberately sinful lives adds insult to injury. This creates the perfect soapbox for Satan to turn our hearts against God: *Look at that guy. He does nothing productive at work, but he was just promoted. Look at her- she committed that crime and got off scot-free. Meanwhile, nothing good is happening to you. Does God really care about you?* When thoughts like these crowd your mind, open a Bible and read Psalm 37 to regain proper perspective. God wants those of us who have been declared righteous in Christ not to be shaken by what is going on around us (Psa. 112:6-7), but instead to give Him thanks in all circumstances (1 The. 5:18).

Trusting in God and waiting on Him, even when we cannot trace Him, are vital for our maturation and sanctification. It forces us to reckon with our faith. We may discover that our faith is too weak to carry us through deep waters. Sadly, some Christians give up rather than engaging in spiritual exercises to strengthen their faith. Commit to being one who works and walks your salvation out. Choose to trust God. You will find that God is renewing your strength as you depend on Him. He will make sure that you do not faint when you are walking. As you start to run, He will not let you grow weary. And when you are ready to fly, He will make you soar like an eagle (Isa. 40:31)! Even if trusting and waiting brings you to your very last breath on Earth, there will be an eternal reward waiting for you in heaven (2 Tim. 4:7).

# Reflections

1. In what areas of my life is my quest for control pushing God out?

2. With what truth, vision, or plan am I struggling to trust God?

3. Which scriptures can I keep in mind as positive affirmation of God's presence and intervention in my life?

4. Who in my life gives me godly counsel? How do I usually receive it?

5. Who in my life is speaking against God's word for my life? How does God want me to respond to this?

6. What kind of spiritual athlete am I? How far am I willing to go to receive all my heavenly rewards?

7. What are my attitude and mindset usually like when I am facing a challenge? Which scriptures will help me adopt and maintain the right perspective?

# A Prayer for You

*Father, I thank you for the person reading this book. Thank you for the life and purpose you have given them. Thank you for revealing to them the awareness of their need for You and for their desire to find You.*

*I pray that they will see You and themselves in a different light.*

*I pray that they will choose to let your Spirit in them guide their mind and subdue their flesh.*

*May they feel their burdens lifted and a lightness in their mind as they confess their sins and forgive others.*

*I pray that they always feel worthy, valued, and heard.*

*May they consider it a privilege, honor, and necessity to communicate with you daily through prayer and praise.*

*I pray that they will trust Your Lordship, wisdom, purpose, and love, waiting joyfully and steadfastly in You.*

*I bring these requests to You, Father.*

*In the name of the Son, Jesus Christ.*

*By the leading of the Holy Spirit.*

*Amen.*

I would love to connect with you in prayer. Please email me at cclpublishco@gmail.com.

# ABOUT THE AUTHOR

**Vanessa Oduah** is a Jesus-loving, people-loving Millennial who strives to live by the mantra of "Christ at the center." Born to a Nigerian family living in the American South, Vanessa pledged her life to Christ at a young age. Two decades (and multiple life lessons) later, she is committed to sharing her stories of tragedy and triumph in an ever-changing relationship with God. Her ongoing mission is to live in a way that keeps God on display as a relevant, stabilizing, and liberating life partner.

In addition to writing, Vanessa enjoys singing, laughing with her siblings, and spending time with her son.

Lightning Source UK Ltd.
Milton Keynes UK
UKHW020940161222
414026UK00010B/1339

9 780578 395418